edited by d-o-t-s
(Laura Drouet, Olivier Lacrouts)

Greenhouse Stories

A Critical Re-examination of Transparent Microcosms

ONOMATOPEE

Under the transept especially,
you forget that there is a roof overhead;
trees, fountains, flower beds and statues...
contribute to the deception that
you are in a garden under the open sky.

quote from an anonymous Russian visitor after viewing the Crystal Palace, in September 1851

Why a Book on Greenhouses Now?

Architecturally speaking, the term 'greenhouse' refers to buildings designed to optimally protect, cultivate and multiply plants under conditions that artificially reproduce their environments of origin. Employed successfully throughout the centuries, these transparent microcosms have allowed some nations to improve their scientific knowledge, provide botanical education to the masses and develop horticultural innovations. Parallel to the benefits they brought with them, however, greenhouses have also had – and keep having – a series of harmful consequences on the way we relate to others (both humans and other-than-humans) and the environments we co-inhabit with them.

Praised for their efficiency and endorsed by governments and companies all around the world, nowadays, industrial greenhouses – in all their different shapes and functions – constitute one of the backbones of our globalised economy. From high-tech commercial glasshouses that produce year-round summer vegetables to nurseries that try to meet the international thirst for exotic houseplants, they are ubiquitous. While they are seen by many as a panacea to satisfy all of humanity's present and future food necessities, one might argue that by freeing us from the constraints of natural cycles – satisfying our desire to have everything *here and now* – modern industrial greenhouses are somehow contributing to our society's desire of increasingly separating ourselves from so-called 'Nature'.

At a time of great anthropocentric pressure on the planet, we believe that looking critically at these [agri]cultural production tools – and questioning the growing use that the agro-industry makes of them – can help us re-establish more humble and meaningful connections with the Earth and its other living communities. Rather than celebrating them as technical prowesses and exceptional architectural feats, this book is an attempt to unveil the multilayered identity of greenhouses, casting light on some of the controversies and opportunities they embed.

Featuring texts by philosophers, growers, anthropologists, activists, scientists, historians and artists from different backgrounds, the following pages propose reflections and suggestions to re-examine these instruments of vegetal containment and domestication from a social, historical, environmental and creative perspective. The commissioned essays and interviews highlight stories of vegetal displacement, colonial appropriation and pollution, but they also help us understand that greenhouses can be fertile spaces for the empowerment of people and the nurturing of socially-engaged and eco-conscious projects.

Echoing anthropologist Dusan Kazic, who – like other 'story makers' such as Anna L. Tsing, Donna Haraway and Vinciane Despret – affirms that "telling stories means making new proposals to imagine new worlds,"[1] this book is an invitation to see greenhouses as incubators for novel and plural narratives. Envisaged as a continuation of the investigations we started with *Plant Fever*,[2] it is intended to encourage us to further "follow the plants,"[3] move away from a human-centred understanding of the world and go beyond the idea that the Earth exists solely for us to use and exploit.

d-o-t-s (Laura Drouet, Olivier Lacrouts)

1 Kazic, D., *Quand les plantes n'en font qu'à leur tête* (Paris: La Découverte, 2022), 105.

2 Drouet, L., Lacrouts, O., eds., *Plant Fever. Towards a Phyto-centred Design* (Hornu/Oostkamp: CID Grand-Hornu/Stichting Kunstboek, 2020).

3 Inspired by Gilles Deleuze and Felix Guattari's essay *A Thousand Plateaus* (1980) which suggests to "follow the plants," anthropologist Natasha Myers explains that encounters with other beings — humans, plants, and even machines — "can incite other ways of seeing, feeling, and knowing. Altered perceptions can destabilize entrenched sensory regimes and bring otherwise imperceptible phenomena within grasp.", in Myers, N., "Sensing Botanical Sensoria — A Kriya for Cultivating Your Inner Plant", Imaginings Series, Centre for Imaginative Ethnography (Vancouver, 2014). ◊ www.academia.edu/6467794/A_Kriya_for_Cultivating_Your_Inner_Plant (Accessed: September 4th, 2019).

Contents

I. Stories to Begin With

Retracing the origins of a 'trouble'[4] can help find a culprit and understand how to deal with it. By contributing to altering our understanding of plants' provenance and morphology, as well as Earth's seasonal cycles, over the centuries greenhouses have nourished the Western idea of 'Nature'[5] as something *separated from* and *to be regulated by* humans. The three essays included in this chapter explore these structures' symbolism and identity, suggesting that greenhouses might be the source of some of today's environmental and social troubles.

4 On the notion of 'trouble', see the book of Donna Haraway, *Staying with the Trouble: Making Kin in the Chthulucene* (Durham, NC: Duke University Press, 2016).

5 In his book *Beyond Nature and Culture*, trans. Lloyd, J. (Chicago: The University of Chicago Press, 2013), French anthropologist Philippe Descola proposes that the idea of 'Nature' as something separate from humans is a Western construct that is not present in all societies.

Cut Off

an essay by d-o-t-s

Ô cloches de verre !
Étranges plantes à jamais à l'abri !
Tandis que le vent agite mes sens au dehors !
Toute une vallée de l'âme à jamais immobile !
Et la tiédeur enclose vers midi !
Et les images entrevues à fleur du verre ![6]

Embodying and at the same time *enabling* innovations, discoveries and renewal – in fields as diverse as engineering, botany, medicine, economy, horticulture[7], and literature[8] – the heated glasshouses that were built in botanical gardens and the private properties of the European nobility and bourgeoisie in the 19th century disorientated even the most travelled of explorers.[9] The illusion they created – a "heterotopia: a space outside the usual constraints of geography, at once all places and none"[10] – made people's heads spin. With their ability to mimic faraway lands[11], their "displays sought to recreate a sense of the exotic atmosphere of the jungles in which many of the plants had originated,"[12] letting visitors safely contemplate them without the "hazards of distant travel: inconvenient locals and alarming animals."[13] Thanks to their polished and transparent accessibility, glasshouses portrayed a "techno-philic utopia, of what the tropical colony might have been had not the 'natural' sloth and sensuous excess of its residents stagnated any progression toward civilizational apotheosis."[14] In parallel with providing spectacle to the masses, their glass structures "symbolized contemporary culture and technology," and greenhouses also rapidly became an "integral part of numerous 19th-century utopian schemes."[15] Recognised by the social hygiene movement as "built, functioning micro Utopias,"[16] they were embraced as "retreats from the real world,"[17] places where the growing number of city dwellers could escape from the polluted air of urban settlements and reconnect with the vegetal world.

As much as they were windows to other worlds, glasshouses also played an important role as vitrines for European empires. By showcasing the diversity of natural resources available in their colonies and how these could be profitably employed,[18] glasshouses highlighted in fact the empires' power and inventiveness serving their global economical, social and civilisational[19] schemes. Thanks to them, the botanical gardens of capital cities like Paris, Brussels and London (among others) became warm receptacles for high economical value plants – such as cacao, pineapple, bananas – freshly transplanted from the colonies and not yet acclimatised to Europe's 'harsh' climate. The "exiled"[20] plants were brought inside and for them to survive, a careful process of rationalisation[21] was put in place. Enclosed in their transparent prisons, protected from outer perturbations (e.g. rain, wind, sun) and isolated from the community of living beings normally entangled to them (e.g. pollinators, fungi, and other microorganisms), selected specimens of the vegetal kingdom were from now on to remain captive under human control and arrangement. And so were the air, the light, the water and the soil that maintained them alive, forming motionless microcosms in which time is suspended.[22] Contained,[23] framed,[24] mastered[25] and altered in the name of rationalisation and science, exotic plants could now be turned into soulless[26] objects for people to observe with relish and for scientists to study them and learn about their secrets. Through this process of alienation,[27] plants were seamlessly transformed into *products*[28] for plantation owners and farmers around the world to grow and multiply. "The trophies of Empire,"[29] also went on to constitute the core of the botanic collections of European institutions that we know of today,[30] keeping greenhouses historically linked to the looting, appropriation and objectification[31] of foreign flora and knowledge perpetrated by colonial powers.[32]

A building that summed up the 19th-century excitement for greenhouses, the fast industrialisation of the Western world, its thirst for novelties and its dreams of expansion was the Crystal Palace. Designed by English architect Joseph Paxton, the famous cast iron and plate glass structure was built to house the technical novelties of the world's leading countries (e.g. England, Belgium, France and Australia) on the occasion of the Great Exhibition that took place in London, England, in 1851. Celebrating British technological excellency, the giant glasshouse stood as a semi-transparent ark, a permeable container full of market-valuable innovations and resources. In his novel *Notes from Underground* (1864), Fyodor Dostoyevsky described the Crystal Palace as a sort of reflexion of a hyper rationalised modern utopia where "everything will be accurately calculated and specified so that there'll be no more actions or adventures left on earth."[33] Drawing from the metaphor of the Russian novelist, in 2014 German philosopher Peter Sloterdijk argued that the Crystal Palace "express[es] the sentiment that the current talk of the 'global market' is ill suited to describing the constitution of life under the spell of obtrusive monetary circumstances. The world interior of the capital is not an agora or a trade fair beneath the open sky, but rather a hothouse that has drawn inwards everything that was once on the outside. The bracing climate of an integral inner world of commodities can be formulated in the notion of a planetary palace of consumption."[34]

Two centuries after their popularisation and the success of Paxton's architectural oeuvre, greenhouses still amaze people, and keep nourishing the utopian dreams of many. While glasshouses in botanical gardens continue to raise awareness about far-off lands and their vegetal richness (with their settings still representing biased versions of so-called 'Nature', and having subtle repercussions on the way we relate to plants out of their context of origin*), a new generation of large-scale greenhouses has fully embraced the principles of vegetal control and planetary consumption. In these new high-tech industrial greenhouses, the processes of rationalisation and objectification of plants — and more generally of all that is alive — initiated in the 19th century have become more sophisticated and intensified.

* In a critical essay on greenhouses,[35] French botanist Yves Delange describes the surprise of the visitor to a tropical greenhouse who fails to identify a *Musa × paradisiaca* (a variety of banana), a plant she is familiar with only in the wild. The *Musa × paradisiaca* in the greenhouse, the visitor highlights, is way bigger than in its natural environment and its leaves are not laciniated as they would normally be under the action of winds. As Delange explains, not being "subject to the action of atmospheric movements," plants growing in greenhouses are "weakened" as "their tissues are not hardened by radiation of a nature comparable to that which is perceived outside."[36] In 2021, a 200 years old *Sabal bermudana* made the headlines of international newspapers. Kept captive at the Royal Botanic Garden Edinburgh, the palm tree had reached the top of the hothouse, 18 metres above ground. For it not to burst through the glass the plant "had been getting shaved for the last decade," reported Angie Brown in an article for the BBC.[37] Interestingly, Brown also noted that the plant had been "self pollinat[ing] as it has both male and female flowers and the opening and closing of doors in the palm house [was] enough passage of air for this to happen." Too tall to be safely removed from the hothouse, in 2021, the Sabal palm finally had to be chopped down due to the restoration works that needed to be done on the building. Seedlings of the same palm were replanted to make up for the disappearance of the elder.

Operating full speed at the service of a galloping productivist agricultural model, which was established in the 20th century and that was further taken up at the beginning of the 21st century, industrial greenhouses seem to have become 'unavoidable' horticultural production tools and are among the pillars of our globalised economy when it comes to food and indoor plants production. The cultivation of crops under permanently built industrial glasshouses keeps expanding globally,[38] and many modern greenhouses are now fully monitored in real-time with hardware devices managing heating, irrigation, air conditioning, LED grow lights and pest control. Often spreading over several hectares of land, these complexes have nothing to do with human-scale farms employing a few polytunnels to complement their cultivation potential. Providing a "divine control"[39] over all sorts of crops, what large-scale industrial glasshouses offer is the guarantee of a year round reliability required by our productivity-driven food system. The Trojan horses of the next (already happening) 'agricultural revolution'[40] – which foresees the full robotisation and digitalisation of the farming world – these colossal greenhouses are also endorsed by agronomists and scientists, who see them as the only tools capable of helping us cope with the ongoing climate crisis and the incessant growth of human population.[41]

Embraced by countries with little to no arable lands such as The Netherlands and Singapore, and by those with harsh climates such as Qatar[42] and Iceland,[43] smart greenhouses are presented as the answer to food insecurity. At a time of global uncertainty (see: repetitive droughts, rising seawater levels, the Russia-Ukraine war, contagious human diseases such as Ebola or COVID-19, and plant pathogens like the *Xylella*) smart greenhouses promise that the physical and economic access to sufficient, safe and nutritious food will be forever granted to everyone. These high-tech structures are also promoted as ways to "preserve the existing resources"[44] as they enable "more land [to] be left for nature"[45] and use less water and less pesticides than in non-covered conventional agriculture. And yet, there are numerous clues – e.g. the shortage of cheap seasonal workforce and the rising costs of gas, electricity, fertilisers, and materials[46] – suggesting that growing/wanting tomatoes for Christmas might not be the wisest idea and that, ultimately, the dream that smart greenhouses present is not as resilient as some tend to argue. Moreover, defying thousands of years of soil-based agriculture in the name of progress, these plant-factories are increasingly advocating for a soil-less cultivation of vegetables, fruits, herbs and microgreens (often highly engineered). Employing human-made substrates such as hydrogel sheets, or water-based nutrient solutions (in the case of hydroponic systems, for instance), they are denying plants the right to spread their roots in soil and remain connected to the pollinators, fungi, and other microorganisms that populate it.

Extensively using the term *hors-sol* (literally 'off the ground'), French contemporary thinkers such as the late Bruno Latour, Malcom Ferdinand and Baptiste Morizot argue that many humans of the Global North have become 'ungrounded', living out of touch with the soil of the Earth and the other living beings that co-inhabit it with us. [46] And yet, the soil is "where food begins."[48] By foreseeing an agriculture fully emancipated from it and that promotes the total regulation of the *Living*, such a productivist system leaves no room for "disturbances"[49] (in the ecological sense of events capable of disturbing or altering an ecosystem). Nor does it allow mutations and collaborations between living communities to happen. At a time of profound crisis of sensitivity[50] for the other-than-human world, what is at stake is our own relationship with the soil. According to the report *Status of the world's soil resources* published by the FAO in 2015, "we know more about soil than ever before, yet perhaps a smaller percentage of people than at any point in human history would understand the truth of this statement. The proportion of human labour devoted to working the soil has steadily decreased through the past century, and hence the experience of direct contact with the soil has lessened in most regions."[51] While still today 95 percent of the food we eat comes directly or indirectly from soils, [52] it could be argued that by emphasising our disconnection from the seasonality of living cycles and the Earth's agrobiodiversity, industrial greenhouses are actively cultivating the emancipation of our own human bodies from the soil in the name of productivity and profitability.

By altering our comprehension of the world and severing our intimate relations to it, over the past two centuries greenhouses have somehow participated in reinforcing Western society's idea of human exceptionalism. The alarming environmental crisis of the last decades, however, has potently reminded us that focusing solely on our species' needs and desires is quickly leading us to a deadend – to the collapse of Earth as we know it. In the time of Climate Change, relying on tools of *climate control* – that cut people off from the 'outside' – can affect our ability to adapt and adjust. What if, instead, our efforts concentrated on reestablishing sensitive and lively relationships [53] with the living world? As American philosopher Donna Haraway reminds us, "we become-with each other or not at all."[54]

NOTES

6 Excerpt of the poem "Cloches de verre", in Maeterlinck, M., *Serres chaudes* (Bruxelles: Paul Lacomblez, 1912).

7 Valen, D., "On the Horticultural Origins of Victorian Glasshouse Culture", *Journal of the Society of Architectural Historians*, Vol 75 No. 4, 2016, 403–23. ◊ www.academia.edu/30232037/On_the_Horticultural_Origins_of_Victorian_Glasshouse_Culture (Accessed: May 16th, 2023).

8 Greenhouses appear regularly in 19th-century novels as torrid or dangerous places where deviant lifestyles are cultivated. e.g.: A plant collector is almost killed in his greenhouse by the bewitching scent of a mysterious orchid in *The Flowering of the Strange Orchid* (1894) by English writer H.G. Wells; A plant conservatory makes a sweaty and exuberant cocoon for two lovers in French writer E. Zola's book *La Curée* (1871); The main character of G. de Maupassant's novel *Un cas de divorce* (1886) describes his sensual passion for the flowers that live inside the "prison" he built for them.

9 "When [...] we look down from the high gallery [...] on the luxuriant reed and tree-like palms below, we feel, for a moment, in a state of complete delusion as to the locality to which we are transported, and we may even believe ourselves to be actually in a tropical climate [...].", words by A. von Humboldt, *Cosmos*, trans. Otté, E. C., 2, 460, in Teltscher, K., *Palace of Palms: Tropical Dreams and the Making of Kew* (London: Picador, 2020), 233-234.

10 "With vegetation gathered from the world over, the Great Stove was a veritable heterotopia: a space outside the usual constraints of geography, at once all places and none.", in Teltscher (2020), 59.

11 Kate Teltscher describes greenhouses as "containers of *other worlds*" in her book *Palace of Palms: Tropical Dreams and the Making of Kew* (2020), 4.

12 Sparke, P., *Nature Inside: Plants and Flowers in the Modern Interior* (New Haven: Yale University Press, 2020), 22.

13 Teltscher (2020), 230-232.

14 Mangione, E. E., "Garden-variety Empire: The Nineteenth-century Glasshouse as Colonial Non-site", *PLATFORM*, August 22nd, 2022. ◊ www.platformspace.net/home/garden-variety-empire-the-nineteenth-century-glasshouse-as-colonial-non-site (Accessed: February 15th, 2023).

15 Ascher Barnstone, D., "Democracy and Glass Construction", *ACSA European Conference* (Berlin, 1997), 227. ◊ www.acsa-arch.org/proceedings/International%20Proceedings/ACSA.Intl.1997/ACSA.Intl.1997.42.pdf (Accessed: January 25th, 2022).

16 Ascher Barnstone (1997), 227.

17 Ascher Barnstone (1997), 227.

18 "The first of its kind, the [Kew's Museum of Economic Botany] aimed to demonstrate the uses of plants, both in their local and global context. The idea had been born out of Hooker's desire to prove the utility of botany and justify the public spending on the Gardens. By demonstrating the multifarious uses of plants, Kew could play its part in stimulating trade and industrial innovation. The nineteenth-century British economy was heavily reliant on plant products, either grown in the colonies or acquired through global trade.", in Teltscher (2020), 240-241.

19 "The transfer of trees across the world, Loudon argued, was a benign form of imperialism: 'it is the beautiful work of civilisation, of patriotism, and of adventure, first to collect these all into our country, and next to distribute them into others... thus contributing almost imperceptibly, but yet most powerfully to the progress and equalisation of civilisation and happiness'.", in Teltscher (2020), 126.

20 "Given Rousseau's disapproval of 'exotic botany', it is not surprising that under cover of a letter of 11 July 1776 he returned Rumphius's *Herbarium amboinense* to the Duchess, while acknowledging it as 'a very precious gift [un cadeau bien précieux]'. He averred, however, that he was not interested in exotic plants 'that we only find among us in exile and altered in the gardens of the curious [qu'on ne trouve parmi nous qu'en exil et dénaturées, dans des jardins des curieux]'", in Cook, A., "Botanical exchanges: Jean-Jacques Rousseau and the Duchess of Portland", *History of European Ideas*, Vol. 33 No. 2, (Milton Park: Taylor & Francis, 2007), 142-156. ◊ www.researchgate.net/publication/222523886_Botanical_exchanges_Jean-Jacques_Rousseau_and_the_Duchess_of_Portland (Accessed: February 10th, 2022).

21 A greenhouse should be the "rational imitation of Nature's laws" ["imitation rationnelle des lois de la nature"], wrote Belgian botanist Paul-Émile De Puydt in his book *Les plantes de serres — Traité théorique & pratique de la culture de toutes les plantes qui demandent un abri* (Mons: Hector Manceaux, 1866), 83.

22 "There was a sense of maternal gathering-in, of the glasshouse overriding the constraints of place and time.", in Mabey, R., *The Cabaret of Plants: Forty Thousand Years of Plant Life and the Human Imagination* (NYC: Norton, 2015), 256.

23 "Plants were not only politically, economically, scientifically and aesthetically controlled in the eighteenth and nineteenth centuries; they were also physically contained in several different ways. Their transportation from the tropics and their cultivation in botanical gardens, commercial nurseries, the private estates of the wealthy and aristocratic, and eventually the conservatories attached to middle-class homes, required them to be enclosed. Whether in cases, orangeries, glasshouses, conservatories, winter gardens or palm houses, plants and flowers experienced levels of containment that they had not known in their natural state.", in Sparke (2020), 19.

24 Sparke (2020), 73.

25 Allain, Y-M., *De l'orangerie au palais de cristal, une histoire des serres* (Saint-Cyr: Editions Quae, 2010), 24-25.

26 Anthropologist Dusan Kazic argues that scientists render plants soulless ["désanimées"] to reduce them to objects dedicated to the production of resources and of study, in *Quand les plantes n'en font qu'à leur tête* (Paris: La Découverte, 2022), 38.

27 We adhere here to Anna L. Tsing's understanding of the term 'alienation': "In capitalist logics of commodification, things are torn from their lifeworlds to become objects of exchange. This is the process I am calling 'alienation'", in *The Mushroom at the End of the World. On the Possibility of Life in Capitalist Ruins* (Princeton: Princeton University Press, 2015), 121.

28 According to North American journalist Michael Pollan, the idea of plants being produced by humans should be questioned as "it makes much sense to think of agriculture as something the grasses did to people as a way to conquer the trees.", in Pollan, M., *The Botany of Desire: A Plant's-Eye View of the World* (New York: Random House, 2001), xxi.

29 "the trophies of Empire", in Mabey (2017), 256.

30 "Much of Kew's work in the 19th century focused on the movement of such plants around the British Empire, which means we too have a legacy that is deeply rooted in colonialism.", in Antonelli, A. "Director of science at Kew: it's time to decolonise botanical collections", *The Conversation*, June 19th, 2020. ◊ theconversation.com/director-of-science-at-kew-its-time-to-decolonise-botanical-collections-141070 (Accessed: September 27th, 2020).

31 "Evocative of colonialist approaches of subjugation and oppression, they [the greenhouses] continue perpetuating the objectification of plants as pure commodities within a capitalist model of production and consumption.", in Gagliano, M., *Thus Spoke the Plant* (Berkeley: North Atlantic Books, 2018), 92.

32 "For hundreds of years, rich countries in the North have exploited natural resources and human knowledge in the South. Colonial botanists would embark on dangerous expeditions in the name of science but were ultimately tasked with finding economically profitable plants. Much of Kew's work in the 19th century focused on the movement of such plants around the British Empire, which means we too [at Kew] have a legacy that is deeply rooted in colonialism.", in Antonelli (2020).

33 Fisher, D. C., "Russia and the Crystal Palace in 1851", in Auerbach, J. A., Hoffenberg, P. H. (eds), *Britain, the Empire, and the World at the Great Exhibition of 1851* (Farnham: Ashgate Publishing Limited, 2013), 138-139.

34 Sloterdijk, P., *In the World Interior of Capital Towards a Philosophical Theory of Globalization* (2014), via Google books (Accessed: May 7th, 2022).

35 Delange, Y-M., "Comment vivent les plantes dans ces maisons en verre ?", in Buchet, A., Delange, Y-M., Allain, Y., Jourda, F., Allorge, L., eds., *Les Serres. Le génie architectural au service des plantes* (Arles: Actes Sud, 2013), 34.

36 Delange, Y-M., in Buchet et al. (2013), 34.

37 ◊ www.bbc.com/news/uk-scotland-edinburgh-east-fife-58650503 (Accessed: November 14th, 2022).

38 "At a global scale, year-round greenhouse vegetable cultivation in permanent or semi-permanent structures (greenhouses or tunnels) is expanding. The total global area covered by greenhouse vegetables was approximately 5.6 million ha in the year 2018 (Cuesta Roble, 2019), with 4.67 million ha or 83% in China (Fei et al., 2018).", in Qasim, W., Xia, L., Lin, S., Wan, L. Zhao, Y., Butterbach-Bahl, K., "Global greenhouse vegetable production systems are hotspots of soil N2O emissions and nitrogen leaching: A meta-analysis" *Environmental Pollution*, Vol. 272, 2021. ◊ www.sciencedirect.com/science/article/pii/S0269749120370615 (Accessed: March 17th, 2023).

39 Hoang, L., Imahashi, R.,, Loh, D., Nagumo, J., Regalado, F., Yiu, P., and Zhou, C., "Asia's new agricultural revolution: planting a high-tech future", *Financial Times*, July 21st, 2022. ◊ www.ft.com/content/3317a430-22b3-4288-b992-c9a8c5d7b920 (Accessed: January 29th, 2023).

40 ◊ www.reporterre.net/Macron-veut-transformer-les-fermes-en-start-up-de-la-tech (Accessed: March 19th, 2023).

41 The world's population is expected to increase by nearly 2 billion persons in the next 30 years, from the current 8 billion to 9.7 billion in 2050 and could peak at nearly 10.4 billion in the mid-2080s. Source: un.org (Accessed: October 15th, 2022).

42 "Qatar is a small country in terms of land area located in the Arabian Gulf with an arid desert climate. The available land and resources are limited; therefore, the country was importing 90% of its food basket products until 2017 (...) Therefore, in the last decade between 2010 and 2019, the greenhouse and open field production of the most consumed vegetables in the country has increased from 31.573 tons to 66.500 tons, recording an approximate 110% increase (...)", in Karanisa, T., Achour, Y., Ouammi, A., Sayadi, S., "Smart greenhouses as the path towards precision agriculture in the food-energy and water nexus: case study of Qatar", *Environment Systems and Decisions*, Vol. 42, (2022), 521–546. ◊ link.springer.com/article/10.1007/s10669-022-09862-2 (Accessed: March 18th, 2023).

43 "Iceland has dramatically reduced the import of fresh vegetables, cutting down on the environmental and financial costs of transportation and preservation. More than 75% of tomatoes, 90% of cucumbers and large proportions of peppers are produced on the island", in "Iceland's innovations to reach net-zero — in pictures", *The Guardian*, December 30th, 2020. ◊ www.theguardian.com/environment/gallery/2020/dec/30/icelands-innovations-to-reach-net-zero-in-pictures (Accessed: March 18th, 2023).

44 Karanisa et al. (2022).

45 Horton, H., "'It's not as carbon-hungry': UK's largest sunlit vertical farm begins harvest", *The Guardian*, October 18th, 2021. ◊ www.theguardian.com/environment/2021/oct/18/its-not-as-carbon-hungry-uks-largest-sunlit-vertical-farm-begins-harvest (Accessed: March 19th, 2023).

46 "The combination of soaring energy bills to provide artificial light to help the plants grow, especially during the winter, combined with associated surges in the price of fertiliser and the cost of packaging prompted many British producers and their European counterparts to take the decision to plant fewer crops this winter.", in Partridge, J., "'We have to pay more for food': Britain's biggest tomato farmer on the runaway costs of growing", *The Guardian*, February 23rd, 2023. ◊ www.theguardian.com/business/2023/feb/23/we-have-to-pay-more-for-food-britains-biggest-tomato-farmer-on-the-runaway-costs-of-growing (Accessed: April 17th, 2023).

47 On the idea of 'soilless humans', see the work of: Ferdinand, M., *Une écologie décoloniale: Penser l'écologie depuis le monde caribéen* (Paris: Seuil, 2019), 139); Morizot, B., *Manières d'être vivant* (Arles: Actes Sud, 2020), 266; Latour, B., "Avoir enfin les pieds sur Terre", Sciences Po, Paris. Supplément climat, hors série, *Le Monde*, novembre 2015.

48 'Soils: Where food begins' was the slogan of the campaign World Soil Day 2022 initially recommended by the International Union of Soil Sciences (IUSS) in 2002.

49 Tsing, A. L., *Il fungo alla fine del mondo, La possibilità di vivere nelle rovine del capitalismo*, trans. Tonoli, G. (Rovereto: Keller, 2021), 236.

50 On the notion of 'crisis of sensitivity', see the work of French philosopher Baptiste Morizot.

51 Status of the world's soil resources, main report, Food and Agriculture Organization of the United Nations (2015). ◊ www.fao.org/3/i5199e/i5199e.pdf (Accessed: March 17th, 2023).

52 "It's alive! Soil is much more than you think.", FAO, September 22nd, 2020. ◊ www.fao.org/fao-stories/article/en/c/1263004/ (Accessed: March 17th, 2023).

53 "Si nous continuons à massacrer cette terre déjà très endommagée, c'est bien parce que nous n'entretenons pas de rapports sensibles et animés avec le monde plus qu'humain.", Kazic (2022), 54.

54 Haraway (2016), 4.

Pôle Nord
Cercle Polaire
Oural
S I B É R
MONGOLIE
IRAN
TIBET
ARABIE
Équateur
OCÉAN INDIEN
PACIFIQUE
OCÉAN

The Golden Spike Is not the Nuclear Bomb*

an essay by Luis Berríos-Negrón

"The movement of energy between enslaved bodies in plantations, plants, long-dead fossilised plants, and industrialised labour is a geochemical equation of extraction in the conversion of surplus. But this radicalised equation of energy is located in a larger field of production and semiotics of extraction. Slavery is not a by-product of this process; rather, slavery is driven by an indifferent extractive geo-logic that is motivated by the desire for inhuman properties. Indigenous genocide and settler colonialism are also part of these extractive geo-logics. In this sense, slavery can be seen not as a confusion of subject – object in relation to inhuman categorisation, but as a total submission to the principle of extraction that was exacted through inhuman differentiation – "transformed from the human subject of his own culture into the inhuman object of the European culture" (Wynter, n.d., 10). The energy regimes that structure material extraction were forced into black material and psychic life – of being energy for others, of putting sugar in the bowl, and in the muscles of white labor; as an "object" of geochemical energy and the rationalization of the black body; as energetic pleasure in all its myriad forms that render the "open and absolute vulnerability" of black and brown bodies to white extraction regimes. Our project is the beginning of asking about this process by which such violent exchanges become possible." [55]

Let's begin by challenging the beginning. I am committed to decolonising the technological history of the greenhouse through arts research. My decolonial research approach is rooted in the forms and forces, the geoaesthetics [56] that shape my life and upbringing on the colony that still is my home-island of Puerto Rico, as part of the broader Caribbean milieu and diaspora. Over time, from that life and research, an intuition emerged, one that led me to sense how the greenhouse strongly represents man's misleading delusion of mastery over, and disconnection from nature. It is from that intuition and ensuing research that I set-forth the following hypothesis: if the greenhouse metaphor embodies the dissociative, colonial reflex driving global warming, then the invention of the greenhouse must be one of the beginnings to the geological timeline of the Anthropocene.

Now, I am aware that since Dutch atmospheric chemist Paul J. Crutzen popularised the remarkable term of *Anthropocene*, many qualified voices have argued for myriad inventions and conditions that might mark the end of the Holocene, and the beginning of Crutzen's Anthropocene – the singular Global Boundary Stratotype Section and Point (GSSP), or 'golden spike' as such a moment is called.[57] At present, the instants and inventions that are suggested to mark the GSSP range from the first stone tool-weapon, to the externalisation of knowledge as written text; and from agriculture itself as practice, to more recent technologies such as the watermill, the steam engine, plastic, and most popularly, the nuclear bomb. That is not to mention the countless calls to rename the epoch itself, with proposals such as the Psychozoicene, Technocene, Capitalocene, Chthulucene, Anthropo-scene, Anthropo-not-seen, etc.[58]

But, while I do definitely subscribe to the virtue of changing nomenclature so to decolonise and transform social injustice, after long consideration, I am also with those who feel that there is no need to rename the Anthropocene, nor mark a singular point or golden spike. On the one hand, I believe that the European-centric prefix *Anthropos* is accurate for the dysfunctions it propels. On the other hand, the marking of a singular moment in time seems suspiciously symptomatic of the commercialising reflex to reduce a needed complexity to a sound-byte morsel for consumption. That is why for me, as a Puerto Rican and Caribbean decolonial observer, the words of geographer Kathryn Yusoff [see opening quote] ring so true. Firstly, because the Caribbean today is at the receiving end of the climate injustices of sea level rise and increasing rate and strength of storms – namely of Atlantic hurricanes (the word 'hurricane' coming from the indigenous *juracán*, the force of chaos and rebirth found between the Taíno ancestral triad of Guabancex, Coatrisquié, and Guataubá). Secondly, because we,[59] in the Caribbean, are the site of the beginning of both the largest genocide and mass human trafficking terrorist scheme in history, mobilised by the old, recalcitrant, industrial-grade greed of the geological and agricultural enterprises.

Therefore, I for one will continue to refuse to accept that the Earth's timeline is for just geologists and stratigraphers to define. Instead, I aim to continue to strengthen the argument that geology and agriculture – as Western sciences – should not be in charge of this particular endeavour. The decolonising of the Anthropocene must continue to be broader and far more comprehensive if it is to serve a greater purpose than merely to further empower one (questionable) discipline. As per Yusoff (and Achille Mbembe, Sylvia Wynter, Noenoe Silva, among many others), what undergirds the core physical and emotional trauma is, if anything, the very colonial gaze of objective observation. It is what sustains the entire extractivist logic, the geologic that drives global warming as the core reflex of capitalism, of Empire, of all fossil fuels. Notwithstanding that, as I write these words, the Anthropocene Working Group (AWG) of the International Subcommission on Quaternary Stratigraphy is currently working to determine that final 'site', the golden spike.

As part of the initial Synapse group (2011) of the Haus der Kulturen der Welt (HKW in Berlin, Germany), I was made aware of, and thereafter attended, several of the scientific conferences, cultural panels, and art exhibitions organised by the HKW around the topic of the Anthropocene (2013-2022), including sessions led by the AWG itself. For me, these events enabled rigorous engagement with two key queries: 1) under whose purview ought the Anthropocene to be defined; and 2) under what disciplinary framework would the point of its beginning be set. The shaping of these queries would from thereon give traction to a plurality of tones, attitudes, and thrusts to deal with the challenges of Global Warming, no less its most awful and enduring violence: hemispheric climate injustice.

With that in mind, during the first days of 2023, I reached out to the executive members of the AWG, Colin Waters and Simon Turner, who are moderating the criteria to select one site that will finally mark that 'beginning' out of a final list of 12 candidate-locations. In my email to them, I contended that they are missing one site: the Specularium, on the Neapolitan isle of Capri, in Italy.

Both Waters and Turner were generous in engaging in discussion. In our exchanges, I first expressed that I do recognise the argument, and rigour for the golden spike to be a stratigraphic marker, as a marker recognisable in the scale and character of geological time. But – as many other voices that the AWG are aware of – I also argued that the criteria for the GSSP ought to be broader. Unfortunately, my proposition was dismissed. Waters and Turner went on to reaffirm the geological framework, unfortunately reflecting back little knowledge about the history of the greenhouse, missing the very essence of the point being made, about greenhouses signifying the final cut that unleashes the delusion of control and dominance over nature and the Earth: "I did not know about the Tiberian greenhouse structure on Capri. A technological fix to cultivate special cucumbers on an island pleasure palace for a paranoid emperor (have just been reading various things online) [...] – who doesn't want to be able to control a microclimate?"[60]

And that is the point. Those of us who stand on the side of enriched and diverse ways to mend our relations with the environment through – among the others – the discourse of the Anthropocene, have failed miserably to communicate how compromised the violent, colonial, misogynist geo-logy of 'climate control' is, and particularly how it is foundational to Western sciences' conception of 'mother Nature'.[61] So, in the spirit of not ceding the ground, and using the same language as critical reflexion, I will summarise here the findings I attained for why the greenhouse as an invention – in the form (and metaphor) of the Specularium – ought to be considered to be a contestant in the GSSP / golden spike pageant.

Generally recognised to be the earliest greenhouse, the Specularium (ca. 34 CE), is itself a stratified site (albeit, in strict disciplinary terms, more archaeological and palaeobotanical, and less geological). As such, I find that it embodies accurately the polemic at hand. Through its mica stone materiality – that is the source of its translucent warming effect, its medicinal-astrological use, and its potently suggestive name in philosophical terms – the Specularium foretells the emergence of the key figure of the Enlightenment – the masculine, self-contained, autogenic man. It marks when Western European humans originally broke away from and began the long-drawn-out technological dissociation from the seasons (ie. from the environment).

No more potent outcome of this fracture is the ensuing, so-called 'Discovery' – really the invasion, raping and sacking – of the Americas. This event, although not so dissimilar in principle from other previous colonial invasions – as a military procedure that occupies and then systematises the unlawful and violent extraction of goods through the enslavement of the conquered – stands out for two overarching reasons: 1) for the unprecedented wealth it had (and continues to produce) for Europe, and others in the Northern Hemisphere; and 2) for the unprecedented scale of the atrocities it had (and continues to produce) against the multitude of Indigenous societies of the Caribbean, and of Central, South and North America, followed by the ensuing kidnapping of entire western and central African civilisations, also for forced labour, torture and murder.

The systematisation of that greed-lathed geo-logy for precious metals and minerals (and later for fossil fuels), becomes a retrograde feedback loop driven by the need to feed the system through agriculture.
This leads not just to the misappropriation of many mineral-, botanical-, medicinal-, and food-production specimens and knowledges, but also to the reflex deforestation of vast areas, for the eventual industrial development and trade of foods and spices (namely tobacco, sugar, coffee, etc.), all underscoring the unfair, unjust, genocidal 'trade' that fuels the Enlightenment, Modernity, and the Anthropocene.

To recognise the greenhouse in this light, one must look deeper, before and after the invasion of the Americas. It remained in the background of horticulture for over a thousand years, where in the early Middle

Ages we find contemporary passages mentioning heated translucent canvas tents, in monastic poems in Italy,[62] and in ancestral cook books in Korea.[63] Later appearances are found in Germanic Europe in the 1500-1600s in massive farmhouse manuals called *Haus Vatter* (literally 'house father') where greenhouses already seem to be a ubiquitous agricultural tool called *Glashaus*,[64] thereon followed by the celebrated *serre* and *orangerie* evolving in 18th-century France.

It is not until the very late 1700s and into the early 1800s that rumblings come from competing experimental work between horticulturists in Great Britain. One of the most prominent rivalries was the one between Scottish botanist John Claudius Loudon and English gardener and designer Joseph Paxton,[65] where they actively designed and tested 'stoves' or 'hothouses', specifically to grow exotic flora out of season, principally to preserve and propagate the bounty of species that had been violently transplanted from the Southern colonies to Great Britain and Europe.

Where the technology of the greenhouse finally reaches its colonial climax is between 1824 and 1851. The greenhouse emerges as a metaphor in 1824, not as agro-technology, but as concept and effect, when French mathematician and physicist Joseph Fourier intuited and proposed that the Earth's atmosphere might act as an insulator of some kind.[66] It was not until 1896, when Swedish physical chemist Svante Arrhenius fully quantified the planetary effect identified by Fourier. In paraphrasing Fourier, Arrhenius stated that "Fourier maintained that [the] atmosphere acts like the glass of a hothouse."[67] Ultimately, it was Swedish meteorologist Nils Gustaf Ekholm who later drew from Arrhenius to coin the planetary misnomer 'greenhouse effect' (misnomer, because the planet does not work like a greenhouse).[68]

In 1834, English doctor Nathaniel B. Ward implements the Wardian case. This staple prototype of agro-technoscience goes from a curious little botanical device and turns into a monstrous industrial infrastructure for transplanting plants. Perhaps most famously, it was used for abducting rubber treelings from Brazil to Loudon's own inspired system of greenhouses at Kew Gardens. It was from Kew that the treelings were then propagated and redeployed to the rest of the colonies of the Empire (including Asia and the Pacific), in order to produce rubber cheaply and increase the wealth of the industry on the backs of the enslaved 'subjects' of the crown.[69]

But the scene of the crime – where it is plain to see the correlation of the global, colonial operation devolving into what today is advanced capitalism – is laid bare to see in all its splendour in the first Great Exhibition of 1851. There, in the grand 17-acre glass greenhouse superstructure that was the Crystal Palace, designed by Paxton to house the Great Exhibition, the technologies of industrial enterprise, as well as the arts and crafts, were put on display prominently alongside the enslaved 'subjects' themselves, as 'human zoos' composed of kidnapped peoples of the colonies.[70]

I do not point to the climax between these key dates so as to demonise the greenhouse, but rather to question the conscious and subconscious contents of the metaphor (as physical psychic and mnemonic complex). The questioning is pursued to destabilise the greenhouse as a colonial tool. The aspiration is that perhaps the decolonial process yields a transformation, turning the tool into a decolonising phenomenotechnic – ie. from the chief, misogynist, racialised container and display of colonial domination, to an uncontained, non-binary support structure that rejects the interior / exterior fallacy and aids in the construction of all kinds of diverse relations and realities for life-affirmation and environmental survival.

I call for the continued decolonising of this technology so as to display not just what ought to be its wise and proportional use, but also how the greenhouse symbolises – and even carries compressed within its transparent surface – the embodied spectral metaphor[71] of all the superrepressed traumata[72] that have come out of the colonial enterprise. This is not just made visible by square kilometres of industrial greenhouse superstructures sprawling in many parts of the world – most famously in Almeria, Spain, and in the second (not the first) *Blade Runner* film – but also by billionaires falling into the untimely mid-life crises of Elon Musk, Jeff Bezos, Richard Branson, et al, and their architects, who are *not* selling rocket ships, but peddling rendered, messianic greenhoused real-estate delusions on the Moon and Mars.[73]

This is why I am not surprised by the images of industrial greenhouses being defaced by environmental stewards, having no choice but to try and bring attention to the climate emergency by means of desperation. Courageous acts by environmental activist groups in France, such as Les Soulèvements de la Terre (The Earth Uprising), may be problematic because they might further empower the unjust policing of climate demonstrators, which is awful enough already. But I fully identify with their frustrated desperation, just as I am frustrated with the narrow view for defining the timeline of the Anthropocene. It is emblematic of how the powerstructures, still, even in the face of all the warnings of climate data, refuse to understand the geological scale of the cataclysm of their greed. Neither the cold scientific objectivity of the unchecked Western technosciences, nor an escapist fantasy of a disposable planet will divert the human species from a near future of extreme heat and cold, of drought and storm, which will inevitably lead, at best, to civil unrest and far-larger forced migrations, core symptoms of climate injustice.

Let me again echo the sentiment of figures like Silva, as well as Hokulani Aikua, Noelani Goodyear-Ka'Opua, and William Ruddiman, among others, who have thoroughly substantiated not just the cultural dimensions that should define the Anthropocene, but that this epoch ought not to be described by one site nor by one Western discipline only. The Anthropocene is very far from *just* being a geological event.

Enough material, not least from inhuman geographers,[74] has already emerged to make it painfully clear that the current geological epoch cannot be merely defined by people who are still trapped in the unchecked, Fordist, European-North American, anthropogenic, still-racist cage that continues lurking to define the conventions of the natural sciences, no less the conventions of a Global Standard Stratigraphic Age. Therefore, as the 'greenhouse' is cascading and collapsing into the 'hothouse' – from the benevolent to the infernal (see below graphic[75]) – it is fundamental to analyse and reconsider the anthropogenic decay mediated by the greenhouse metaphor and its semiotic of colonial memory.

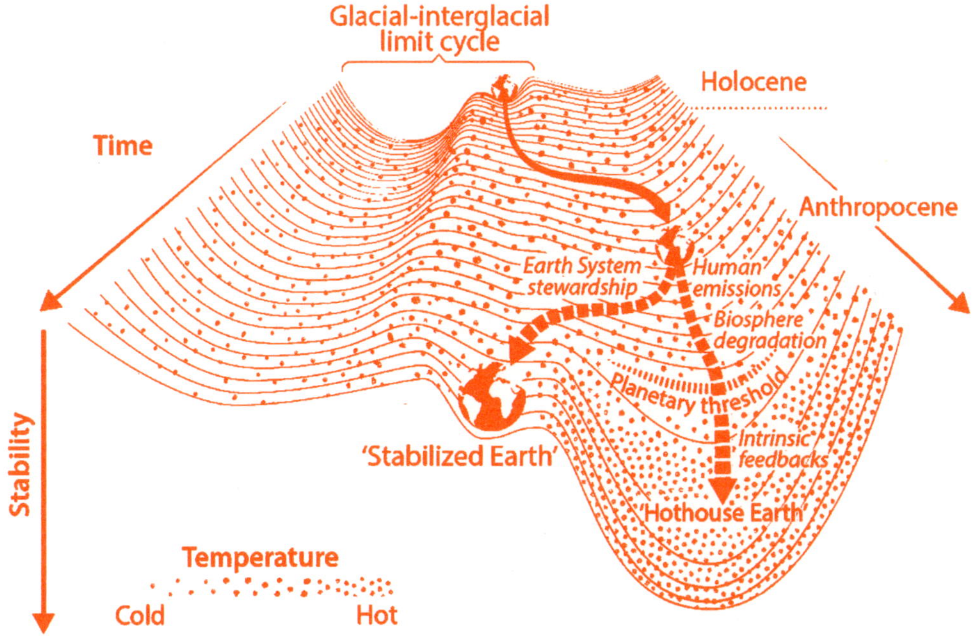

DISCLAIMERS

* This text – the full title of which is "The Golden Spike Is not the Nuclear Bomb: Propædeutic to the Paramannerist Treatise" – is the third chapter of a broader reflection and follows the short science fiction entitled "One Micron a Light-year Ago into Thirdness: Fictions from the Paramannerist Treatise" and the conference paper and essay "Manners, Parameters, and the Gay Sciences: Realities from the Paramannerist Treatise". In 2011, while in the Huancayo province of Peru weaving the rugs I would show at Documenta13, I was commissioned by architect Nadin Heinich to write a short story for her book *Digital Utopia* (Akademie der Künste, 2012). In the altitude delirium of coca leaves I wrote "Fictions...". Later that year, I was kindly invited to present a paper at a conference at the Hochschule für Künste Bremen. That paper presentation became the essay "Realities..." later published in the book *Rauchwolken und Luftschlosser* edited by conference organisers Andrea Sick & Dennis Paul (Textem Verlag, 2013). "Fictions..." was translated and reprinted in German in the catalogue *Planet B – Ideas for a New World* (Verlag der Buchhandlung Walther Konig, 2016) edited by curator Alain Bieber for the eponymous exhibition at the NRW Forum in Düsseldorf; "Realities..." was reprinted in *Space Matters: Exploring Spatial Theory and Practice Today* (Ambra Verlag MMag. Franz Schaffer, 2013) edited by curator Lukas Feireiss as a follow-up document to the conference he conducted of the same title at the University of Art and Design in Linz in 2013. I mention this in order to give context to why this contribution is the third instalment of the Paramannerist Treatise. Also, I want to describe why I lean on Lina Bo Bardi's use of the term 'propædeutic', one that led her to intensify her condemnation of the divisions driven by ideologies of interior and exterior – physically, spatially, and mentally – perhaps as the chief deformation of living imposed upon the Americas. Like Bo Bardi, I look to activate a propædeutic of provocations against the inadequacies of technocratic methodologies and modernism's penchant for 'scientificism'. Moreover, I look to echo and manifest her *modus operandi* of work she called 'immediate-life-architecture' to be contrasted against a cogent idea of environment as 'total-space' where practice is not spectacle or spectator, but the deployment of spaces that operate as "*organisms apt for life*". With this latest *addendum* to the Paramannerist Treatise (commissioned specifically by the editors of this publication) I look to prolong an evolving series of position-takings that reflect my insistence upon the political strengths of Tropical Modernism, as an epoch that, like Mannerism, must be retrospectively assigned in order to playfully end – and unleash us from – North-Western modernity and its toxicities, not necessarily through a technoscientific 'parametricism', but perhaps through a revised parametric determinism (see Ernst Mandel) for decolonial endeavour.

** All references in this text are referenced in my dissertation *Breathtaking Greenhouse Parastructures: A Supplement to the Arcades Project from a Caribbean Perspective (and a Call to a Careful Practice of Epistemológica)* (2015-20, 796). It is my doctoral dissertation for the Art Technology Design PhD Programme between Konstfack University of Arts Crafts & Design and the Royal Institute of Technology (KTH) of Sweden. It is a work of research based on art methodologies. It pertains to the genres of installation, environmental art, and social science fiction. As such, it offered no solutions. In fact, it is part of the problem. And that is the thrust... it is a practise-based research effort, shaped through my Caribbean perspective, that evolves into an indirect metanarrative working in the service of complexity, uncertainty, and speculation. The main site of that reflexive process is the book. And what you will find is an experimental treatment of the technology of 'greenhouse' presented as a boundary object for marginal discursive and sculptural studies. Through it we will 'walk' so to (re)mediate the see- mingly-inescapable destiny of Global Warming. That iterative, and at times repetitive metaphorical walk is formatted to question how 'greenhouse' (dis)embodies the spectres of colonial memory that drive Global Warming; and to offer a diverse deposition of 'greenhouse' that is life-affirming, rather than messianic or toxic. The book itself is a prop, a theatrical object for inquiry and reflexion; it is a proportional supplement to Walter Benjamin's unfinished opus *The Arcades Project [Das Passagen - Werk]*; and it is a propeller encouraging specialists and experts to address Global Warming as the complex of modern psycho-social afflictions that continues to affect all other disciplines (particularly technological history and the natural sciences). Remember: so to address that manifold-complex from a transdisciplinary (if undisciplinary) set of positions, *Breathtaking Greenhouse Parastructures* will always ask to be open to be read, observed, and perceived from various positions, orders and directions.

NOTES

55 Yusoff, K., *A Billion Black Anthropocenes or None* (Minneapolis: University of Minnesota Press, 2018), 25-26.

56 la Cour, E., *Geo-Aesthetical Discontent: Svalbard, the Guide and Post-Future Essayism*, Documented Artistic Research Project (Doctoral Thesis) in Artistic Practice at HDK-Valand – Academy of Art and Design, University of Gothenburg Art Monitor 90 dissertation, Göteborg 2022.

57 Waters, C. N. et al., "Candidate Sites and Other Reference Sections for the Global Boundary Stratotype Section and Point of the Anthropocene Series", *The Anthropocene Review*, Vol. 10 No. 1, April 2023, 3–24. ◊ DOI.org (Crossref), ◊ www.doi.org/10.1177/20530196221136422.

58 Various references here, but mainly see Hui, Y., Lemmens, P., "Reframing the Technosphere: Peter Sloterdijk and Bernard Stiegler's Anthropotechnological Diagnoses of the Anthropocene", *Krisis Journal for Contemporary Philosophy*, No 2, 2017, 25-41.

59 The 'we' here represents a careful way for me, as Antillean Puerto Rican (now of the diaspora), not to compare or claim to speak for all in the Region, but to associate myself to the broader challenges we face as an Antillean community in regards to the climate injustices of sea-level rise and intensified hurricanes, storms and droughts. It also represents how I aspire carefully to associate with those who are concerned and want to change the toxic behaviours driving global warming through action, not technoscience.

60 Turner, S., in email conversation also with Waters, C., January 1st-12th, 2023.

61 See arguments made by Sofia, Z., in "Container Technologies", *Hypatia*, Vol. 15 No. 2, 2000, 181, and by Marisol de la Cadena, Donna Haraway, D., and Eduardo Viveiros de Castro, in Adamson, J. and Galeano J. C., "Why Bears, Yakumama (Mother of All Waters), and Other Transformational Beings Are (Still) Good to Think: Humanities for the Environment.", with illustrations by Solmi Angarita, *Humanities for the Environment, Ecocentricismand Indigenous Studies*, (New York and London: Routledge, 2016), 226.

62 See mentions of early light cover-structures (*Giardini Relativi Alle Stagione*), winter housings (*Delle Citroniere*) in Alamanni, L., *La Cultivazione* (Bassano: a Spere Remondini di Venezia, 1795).

63 Yoon, S. J., Woudstra, J., "Advanced Horticultural Techniques in Korea: The Earliest Documented Greenhouses", *Garden History*, Vol. 35 No. 1, (The Gardens Trust, 2007), 68–84.

64 Glasshouses are already described as 'common' among the aristocratic farm landlords of Prussian Pomerania. See: *Grosser Herren Stands und adelicher Haus-Vatter. Christoph Riegels seel. Wittib und Erben, Frankfurt am Oder und Leipzig* (1719) 954. Source courtesy of Stiftung Bibliothek Werner Oechslin.

65 Colquhoun, K., *A Thing in Disguise: The Visionary Life of Joseph Paxton* (New York City: Harper Perennial, 2004).

66 Fourier, J-B. J., "On the Temperatures of the Terrestrial Sphere and Interplanetary Space / Mémoire de l'Académie Royale Des Sciences de l'Institute de France. 7", in Archer, D., Pierrehumbert, R., *The Warming Papers: The Scientific Foundation for the Climate Change Forecast*, 1824/2011, 7–20) 7 (1824), 569 (2011).

67 Arrhenius, S., "On the Influence of Carbonic Acid in the Air upon the Temperature of the Ground", *Philosophical Magazine and Journal of Science*, Ser. 5 Vol. 41, April 1896, 241.

68 Christianson, G.E., *Greenhouse: The 200-Year Story of Global Warming* (New York City: Walker and Company, 1999).

69 See Keogh, L., "The Wardian Case: Environmental Histories of a Box for Moving Plant", *Environment and History*, Vol. 25 No. 2, May 2019, 219–44; and Maylack, J., "The Wardian case made intercontinental plant transport possible—and helped spread empires. An Object Lesson", *The Atlantic online*, November 12th, 2017. ◊ www.theatlantic.com/technology/archive/2017/11/how-a-glass-terrarium-changed-the-world/545621/ (Accessed: January 25th, 2023).

70 See Helmreich, A., "On the Opening of the Crystal Palace at Sydenham, 1854", *BRANCH: Britain, Representation and Nineteenth- Century History. Ed. Dino Franco Felluga. Extension of Romanticism and Victorianism on the Net*, 2012. ◊ www.branchcollective.org/?ps_articles=anne-helmreichon- the-opening-of-the-crystal-palace-at-sydenham-1854 (Accessed: August 15th, 2015). And Sánchez-Gómez, L. A., "Human Zoos or Ethnic Shows? Essence and Contingency in Living Ethnological Exhibitions", *Culture & History Digital Journal*, Vol. 2 No. 2, December 2013, 22.

71 Peeren, E., *The Spectral Metaphor: Living Ghosts and the Agency of Invisibility* (London: Palgrave Macmillan, 2014).

72 Derrida, J., *Archive Fever: A Freudian Impression*, trans. Prenowitz, E., (Chicago: University of Chicago Press, 1995/2008), 79.

73 An example is the Mars projects developed by architecture studio Bjarke Ingels Group for the UAE. See: Koronka, P., "Architects have designed a Martian city for the desert outside Dubai", *CNN online*, June 10th, 2020. ◊ www.cnn.com/style/article/mars-science-city-design-spc-scn/index.html.

74 Inhuman geography is a specific discipline. To learn more, see the work of Yusoff ◊ www.qmul.ac.uk/geog/staff/yusoffk.html.

75 "Stability landscape showing the pathway of the Earth System out of the Holocene and thus, out of the glacial-interglacial limit cycle to its present position in the hotter Anthropocene. The 'fork in the road' is shown here as the two divergent pathways of the Earth System in the future (broken arrows). Currently, the Earth System is on a Hothouse Earth pathway driven by human emissions of greenhouse gases and biosphere degradation toward a planetary threshold at ~2 °C, beyond which the system follows an essentially irreversible pathway driven by intrinsic biogeophysical feedback. The other pathway leads to Stabilized Earth, a pathway of Earth System stewardship guided by human-created feedbacks to a quasi-stable, human-maintained basin of attraction. 'Stability' (vertical axis) is defined here as the inverse of the potential energy of the system. Systems in a highly stable state (deep valley) have low potential energy, and considerable energy is required to move them out of this stable state. Systems in an unstable state (top of a hill) have high potential energy, and they require only a little additional energy to push them off the hill and down toward a valley of lower potential energy.", in Steffen, W., Rockström, J., Richardson, K. et al., "Trajectories of the Earth System in the Anthropocene", *Proceedings of the National Academy of Sciences — PNAS*, Vol. 115 No. 33, August 2018, 8254.

Trappings of the Greenhouse

Prudence Gibson in conversation with Monica Gagliano and Michael Marder

Monica Gagliano, Prue Gibson and Michael Marder all conduct research in the field of Critical Plant Studies and have worked together on various projects, papers and books. This conversation between the three scholars focuses on the greenhouse as a complex concept, object, site and place of vegetal practice.

Prudence Gibson I want to ask you both about a hypothesis: that over the last few thousand years humans have traced a full Edenic Circle. The Edenic narrative suggests that after being evicted from the Garden of Eden, humans have been striving to return to the garden. While it is true that this striving has been exacerbated by imperial and colonial mastery of the wilderness, we are now at a stage where gardens are the only answer. I wonder if there has been a return to the idea of the greenhouse in a similar way?

Michael Marder Strange as it may sound, we do come full circle back to the Garden of Eden as a sort of nightmarish reality in the guise of the greenhouse. In saying this, I am very much thinking about and agreeing with St. Hildegard of Bingen [Ed: *the twelfth-century abbess and polymath*]. For Hildegard, the first humans, Adam and Eve, are created plant-like out of the earth and they imbibe their *viriditas* [Ed: *a term coined by Hildegard to express the notion of a "greening power of God" – a divine creative force that, according to her, is visible in the lushness and greenness of nature*] directly from the earth. They live in the Garden of Eden, like two greenhouse plants really, until they are expelled from it. That is when their connection to the earth, and, through it, to the self-refreshing power of creation, is cut.

Well, Hildegard sets up her ecological theology in terms of a standoff between *viriditas* and *ariditas*, where *ariditas* refers to anything that goes against life itself, that rigidifies boundaries and imposes the *rigor mortis* of an identity – it is the aridity, the scorching heat that emanates from what we might call sin, but without any moralistic overtones. So the whole drama of Hildegard's theology unfolds between the two poles of *viriditas* and *ariditas*. Now, we might say that the age of Global Warming is the age of increased *ariditas*. Greenhouse effects are produced by these fallen human-plants who are no longer plant-like and who are creating a terrifying greenhouse that is planet-wide. So, there is indeed a return to the greenhouse, though no longer in its initial Edenic state, but precisely as the opposite, replete with deadening greenhouse gases.

Monica Gagliano I wonder if that is also because by being so desperate to return home, we have not understood where home actually is: always there, under our feet and in our body. Instead, we are trying to find home in some old, lost imaginary places. And we have created this artificial greenhouse-home, which is trying to expel us like we got expelled from the greenhouse of the Garden of Eden. Being expelled for misbehaviour: it seems we are repeating the same pattern now, as if it were a modern version of the original sin.

MM Yes. And, of course, everything accompanying the expulsion is important. The punishment meted out by God is hard labour – both in the sense of physical work and of giving birth. Morethan that, death is given as punishment and is put in terms of a return to the earth: Adam and Eve were crafted out of the earth, to which they return. What we have here is a homecoming in death, basically.

MG True, and our global greenhouse does not appear to protect us as a normal greenhouse would be expected to. If anything, it is just reminding us that the only way out is by dying. And this death does not necessarily have to be the physical death of human bodies, it can be the death of the society that we have created.

PG Going back to the original 'idea' of the greenhouse: would you say that it is still related to a place of productivity, economic botany, and of social value?

MM The greenhouse detaches plants from the places where they used to grow, but also from the time of growth and seasonality. Thanks to the greenhouse, you can extend the time propitious to growth or you can play with it in different ways. And this decontextualization is something that, at a certain point, humans have started doing to themselves, as well as to other-than-human beings. Decontextualization is really dis-embeddedness, which, to my mind, is the strongest sense of artificiality.

MG And what is also interesting is that, for the plants to grow in greenhouses, these have to be made of transparent materials like glass. Their transparency is a kind of pretending that the space is open and natural, and that you are in the right place and should not worry. It is interesting that what we do to plants in greenhouses, we do to ourselves in the global greenhouse we have locked ourselves in. We use the greenhouse as an apparently optimal environment to make plants do things that they normally would not. And we do the same with ourselves.

MM Absolutely and I would say that there is something fundamentally ambivalent about the greenhouse. On the one hand, it is a figure of the production and instrumentalised reproduction of plant life, and, on the other hand, it is a figure of care. A greenhouse plant is essentially a plant that is meticulously cared for and that is protected from the outer hostile elements.

PG Yes, in a greenhouse everything has to be enhanced and improved for human consumption. There is a culture of growing plants in larger size, for larger numbers of people and there is a sense of doing research for more economic gain and growth. But then there is also the aesthetics of the greenhouse, right? I find the greenhouse at the Royal Botanical Gardens in Sydney very romantic, for instance. There is often steam and misty water, and you move through a space where you cannot see clearly, the smells are quite manky and the floor is wet: somehow it is a place of discovery. I wonder if the aesthetic experience of seeing greenhouses in the landscape is something to consider too?

MG A place that I find interesting in that sense is the Eden Project, in the UK. It is located on a piece of land that was manicured and it looks amazing from an aesthetic perspective. There are these domes that stick out of the landscape, but they also fit in it— it is strange. And when you enter the space, it is exactly what you described, Prue. The environment is designed to be fully tropical, so you go from the English, cool and fresh, air to a jungle. They are growing tropical plants in there and it looks very lush. But then the question is: "What is the work that is required to maintain that jungle?" Clearly, England is not the tropics. So how much energy is required to even run and create an environment that size in the wrong place? There is this illusion of the greenhouse as a very healthy, nourishing and flourishing space, but a lot of work is demanded to maintain that romantic ideal look.

PG When I was at the Temperate House in Kew Gardens, London, a few years ago, I also thought about the structure of the greenhouse there, which is basically made of framed glass, hence creating the idea of a device for framing the plants and aestheticizing them. The greenhouse acts like a cabinet of curiosity and carries out a sort of imperial dominion over plants. And then you have the Eden Project, which has these biospheres and the rhetoric there is more like: "This can be our future. We can all live safely in here without the sun and we will be protected from everything."

MM It seems to me that the biospheres or bio-domes are, in fact, experiments in climate engineering, which is the prevalent technological response to the climate disaster. People have the tendency to think: "If there is a problem, we will just engineer the right climate." As if we could deal with global climate changes in the same way that we regulate the temperatures in our houses. It obviously does not work that way. Maintaining what is within the dome requires lots of energy and emissions. A controlled environment is there because there is uncontrollable change brewing outside of it.

PG I think it would be interesting to hear about any experiences you have had with greenhouses.

MG Personally, I have conducted experiments in greenhouses and the idea was exactly to try having a pseudo-natural environment. One of my experiments involved peas, which are cold temperature plants and love being between 16°C and 18°C. They do not grow in the hot 30°C of Australia, for instance. The greenhouse we used was equipped with fans that were supposed to keep the space cool. But ultimately, after a certain time, the peas would stop germinating and growing and I had to halt the experiments. By stopping, the plants were somehow saying: "No. We are not participating in this." And this takes me back to thinking about greenhouses as the quintessential places where we objectify plants. The same way that zoos objectify animals. We bring them all to us where we can meet them under our own terms. And we are also assuming that those animals and plants are behaving just normally. We are assuming that the botanic gardens, for example, are places where we meet plants. Well, we are not meeting plants. We are meeting a representation of them in a total human-constructed way, a theatre of what plants could vaguely be. And I think that is why these places are so problematic: because they are a theatre of horror really.

MM Yes, there is something pernicious about the transparency of the greenhouse and its apparent capacity to supply all the material conditions of possibility for life and for thriving. It seems like it is an act of generosity: giving enough light and the right temperature, the right soil, humidity levels... But at the same time, the greenhouse can be seen almost as a symbol of the liberal or neoliberal paradigm of giving life under instrumental conditions. Giving life, but only in exchange for productivity and reproductivity. In my mind, I see a relation between the greenhouse and Antigone's cave. When Creon puts Antigone in a cave [Ed: *in a scene from the play by the classical Greek writer Sophocles*] – in a kind of closed environment – he seals her off from the rest of the world. He does not take her life away with his own hands directly, but does so by denying her connection to the elements, to the world. It is an indirect killing through her separation from a livable environment. A greenhouse, then, is a modified Antigone's cave in which the walls are not opaque but transparent. Seemingly, the conditions of possibility for life are granted, but on the strict condition, that, "You will perform, produce and reproduce the way I want you to."

MG And I guess the neoliberal thread connects to the beginning of our conversation, and to the idea of the greenhouse as a tool with which we can say to plants: "I am giving you all of these luxurious, comfortable conditions to live in. You just have to do what I say and not worry about the consequences" – which are actually deadly. So there is a process of taking the life, even in this context. And, also, the conclusion to which one might come is that the only possibility for survival is inside the greenhouse because outside of it, the conditions are lethal. So again, the theatre of life-giving and life-taking seems to be playing quite a lot in a greenhouse. With the addition of the glass separating the inside and the outside and which attempts to make the two realities difficult to distinguish.

MM It is really a staging of sovereignty in the biopolitical paradigm, sovereignty not only over life but specifically with regard to plants, over what determines their being, which is what Aristotle calls the Threptikon – the nourishing and reproductive soul [Ed: *in his treatise 'De Anima' written about 350 BC*]. That is what is being determined there: the ontological core of the plant that is being reduced on the whim of capital. It is the time of agro-capitalism and of the reproduction of economic value that takes over the seasonality and the time of plant growth and reproduction.

MG Correct. And also, I was thinking about what you shared before we started recording, Prue, when you said something about how greenhouses and gardening are kind of connected. But I think that there is a big difference. To garden, you have to submit to the rules and they are not the ones you have made. That is why I think gardening is really about co-creating. There is this connection to the earth that can dictate what can and will grow and you are just supporting that... So, when you garden, you have to adapt to the seasons so that things can grow.

And sometimes they still do not grow, but that is okay, you cannot force them. It requires a dialogue between you and the garden which cannot be manicured too much. I think that the relationship is very different between co-creating a space with the land itself in the garden or enslaving plants in an environment like a greenhouse which is not truly conducive for their growth and health because it forces their growth and reproduction out of season.

MM I agree, Monica, we ought to consider greenhouses and gardens in relation to the places of plants. Because plants are of a piece with the places where they are. What greenhouses enable, compared to gardens, is the portability of places: with greenhouses, not only can specific beings be displaced, but entire places too can become portable.

MG Yes, and in that sense, the greenhouse embodies a sense of placelessness because it actually is a no place.

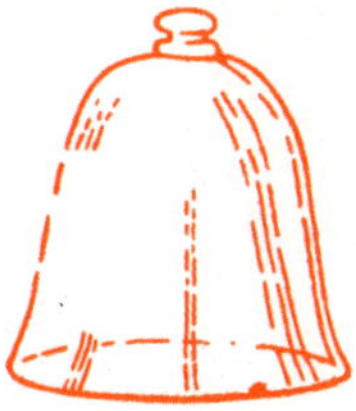

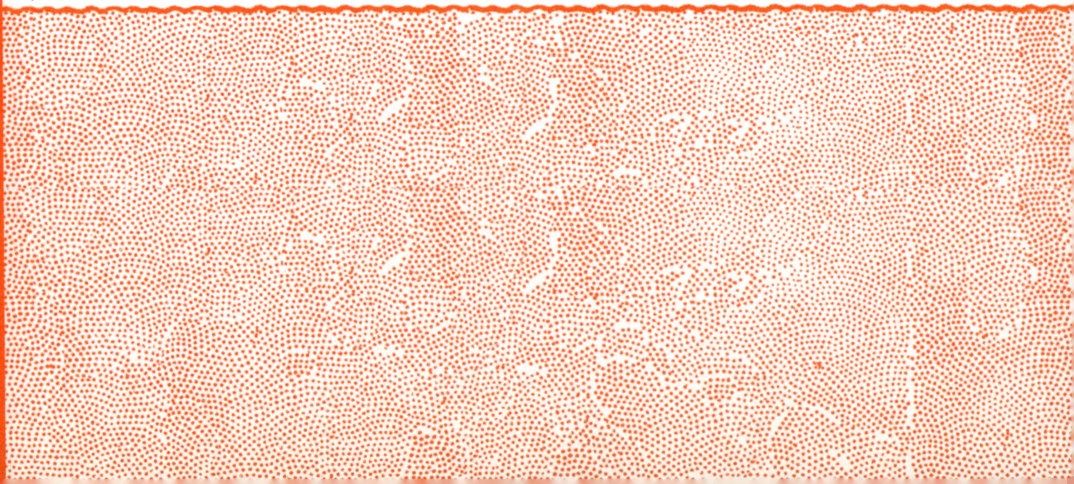

II. Old Stories

As containers for the contemplation and appreciation of foreign flora, over time greenhouses participated in cultivating people's dreams, imagination, and knowledge — but also fears and stereotypes — about both the plants they enclosed and the places such flora came from. From travelling plants to myths and the empowerment of women, the following essays propose three different perspectives on the history of greenhouses deconstructing and questioning the role they played in society.

Plant Horror in the Palm House at Kew

an essay by Kate Teltscher[76]

The opening sequence of Steve Sekely's 1962 science fiction film, *The Day of the Triffids*, features a dramatic meteor shower over London. Orange flashes illuminate the familiar silhouette of Kew's Palm House against the night sky. The meteors carry the seeds of triffids, monstrous man-eating plants. One finds its way into the Palm House, where it grows at exponential rate and, even more alarmingly, starts to stir. The triffid stalks and then strikes down the terrified Palm House nightwatchman. Originally published as a novel by John Wyndham in 1951, *The Day of the Triffids*, in its various textual and screen incarnations, occupies a prime position in the subgenre of plant horror, tales of death-dealing plants which became popular from the late nineteenth century.[77] Critics generally locate the origins of plant horror in Charles Darwin's research into carnivorous plants and plant mobility, in particular his publication of *Insectivorous Plants* (1875) and *The Power of Movement in Plants* (1880).[78] But stories of murderous plants have been associated with Kew's Palm House since its inception, decades before the publication of Darwin's influential works.

76 My thanks to Felix Driver for his helpful comments on this article.

77 Miller, T. S., "Plants Monstrous", in Weinstock, J. A., ed., *The Ashgate Encyclopedia of Literary and Cinematic Monsters* (London: Routledge, 2016), 472.

78 See for instance Blake-Price, C., "Vegetable Monsters: Man-Eating Trees in Fin de Siècle Fiction", *Victorian Literature & Culture*, Vol. 41 No. 2, (2013), 312; Chang, E., "Killer Plants of the Late Nineteenth Century", in Karpenko, L. and Claggett, S., *Strange Science: Investigating the Limits of Knowledge in the Victorian Age* (Michigan: University of Michigan Press, 2017), 87; Keetley, D., Tenga, A., eds., *Plant Horror: Approaches to the Monstrous Vegetal in Fiction and Film* (London: Palgrave Macmillan, 2016), 17; Endersby, J., *Orchid: A Cultural History* (Chicago: Chicago University Press, 2016), 142-5; Desmarais, J., *Monsters under Glass: A Cultural History of Hothouse Flowers from 1850 to the Present* (London: Reaktion, 2018), 167; Smith, J., "Darwin's plants and Darwin's Gardens: Sex, Sensation and Natural Selection", Chap. 6, in Edney, S., ed., *Ecogothic Gardens in the long 19th Century* (Manchester: Manchester UP, 2020).

READING SUGGESTION

Edited by scholar of Gothic and Horror literature Daisy Butcher, *Evil Roots – Killer Tales of the Botanical Gothic* is a British Library Tales of the Weird collection of short stories from 1844 to 1932 starring killer plants. Among them is a short story by H. G. Wells, about a deadly orchid emitting a bewitching "rich intensely sweet scent, that overpowered every other in that crowded, steaming little greenhouse". Butcher claims that "these fantasies provide a sense of repercussion when nature fights back".

The Palm House was completed in 1848, the first building to be commissioned after the botanic gardens transferred from royal to public ownership. From the start, the building attracted considerable attention from journalists and the popular scientific, educational and religious press. But if, on the one hand, the palm display presented the audience with a magnificent spectacle of tropical luxuriance and abundance, Kew's collection also contained some more menacing aspects. The Palm House constituted a thrilling site of colonial fear with plant horrors lurking in the undergrowth. With its humid heat and unfamiliar vegetation, it offered visitors a simulacrum of the tropics and, more specifically, of the colonies. Slavery had been abolished in most British colonies just fifteen years before the Palm House opened. The plants, supplied by colonial botanic gardens across the world, told stories of British colonial expansion, missionary activity, extraction and cultural encounter. Amongst the collection were economically significant food crops, such as sugar, which inevitably evoked enslaved plantation labour and its attendant cruelties. Other specimens were associated with indigenous practices which European observers construed as superstitious and barbaric. Poison plants were objects of equal fascination and repulsion.

As historian David Arnold has documented in *Toxic Histories: Poison and Pollution in Modern India*, the British in India were haunted by the fear of poisons and the need to gain knowledge about their source and operation.[79] The Palm House provides us with a way to explore the violence implicit in many nineteenth-century plant narratives.

One of the express aims of Kew Gardens was public education. Sir William Hooker, Kew's first director, issued a sixpenny illustrated guide, *Kew Gardens* (1847), which went through numerous editions and furnished material for newspaper and journal articles, guidebooks and cheap educational texts. Hooker augmented the botanical information with extracts from poetry. A number of the poetic descriptions of plants were taken from Mary Russell Mitford's romance, *Christina, the Maid of the South Seas* (1811). While Hooker did not acknowledge his source, the poem was popular in its day, and would have been recognised by a section of his readership. The poem was particularly appropriate to Kew. *Christina* was set on the South-Pacific island of Pitcairn, home to a small community established in 1790 by mutineers from *HMS Bounty* and a group of Tahitians. *HMS Bounty* had been engaged on a voyage to transfer the breadfruit from Tahiti to the West Indies; a scheme to provide food for the enslaved population, proposed by Sir Joseph Banks, the unofficial director of Kew. Hooker touched on this scheme by quoting Mitford's description of the breadfruit's sustaining qualities: "The tree, which in unfailing stores, / The staff of life spontaneous pours" (Canto 2, v. 10).[80] However, as a writer of abolitionist sympathies, Mitford disapproved of the plan to use breadfruit to support plantation slavery. Hooker once again cited *Christina* in his account of sugar cane, but introduced the quotation with a reminder that the British had abolished slavery in their colonies: "*Sugar Cane*... happily can be no longer denounced,

79 Arnold, D., *Toxic Histories: Poison and Pollution in Modern India* (Cambridge: Cambridge University Press, 2016), Chaps. 2, 3.

80 Hooker, W. J., *Kew Gardens, or A Popular Guide to the Royal Botanic Gardens of Kew* (London: Longman, Brown, Green & Longmans, 1852), 26.

with regard to this country, as 'The cane whose luscious juice supplies / Europe's blood-purchased luxuries'" (Canto 1, v. 10).[81] With this brief preface, Hooker performed a textual act of disavowal: both alluding to, and distancing Britain from, the cruelties of its recent slaving past.[82]

The evangelical naturalist, Philip Henry Gosse, more directly foregrounded plantation brutality in *Wanderings through the Conservatories of Kew* (1857). Issued anonymously by the Society for Promoting Christian Knowledge, *Wanderings* was part of the mid-nineteenth-century venture to supply cheap religious texts on scientific subjects. Gosse's distaste for slavery is evident in *Wanderings*' description of the dumb cane (*Dieffenbachia seguine*), a species native to the Caribbean. Readers were informed that the plant gained its name from its juice "so acrid as to inflame the lips and tongue that touch it, swelling the parts so as to take away the power of speech." The plant had notoriously been used as a "means of torture" on enslaved people in British colonies. Gosse reported that a Kew gardener who once "incautiously bit a piece of the dumb cane" was unable to speak, and was "in the most excruciating torments" for days.[83] In this manner, the plant itself brought home the guilt, and exacted a form of retribution, for the brutalities of slavery.

For the most part, however, the plants in these Victorian texts told stories of the inhumanity of indigenous people. In the entry for tanghin (*Cerbera manghas*) or the '*Poison Tree* of Madagascar', for example, Hooker mentioned "the execrable laws of the Malagassy kingdom." In a footnote, he directed readers to an article in his own *Botanical Miscellany* (1833).[84] The missionary accounts that Hooker printed in the *Botanical Miscellany* provided the material for Gosse in his

81 Hooker (1852), 24.

82 For the idea of disavowal, see Hall & Pick (2017).

83 Gosse, P. H., *Wanderings through the Conservatories at Kew* (London: Society for Promoting Christian Knowledge, 1857), 118.

84 Hooker (1852), 27.

description of the use of tanghin in Madagascan trials by ordeal. According to the missionary accounts, when a crime was detected, the highly poisonous seeds of tanghin were used to determine an individual's guilt or innocence. A small quantity of pounded tanghin seed was administered to a suspect. If it caused vomiting, the individual was deemed innocent; if death ensued, the individual was declared guilty. Compared to dumb cane, Gosse observed, tanghin was a "poison, still more deadly and of more infamous celebrity."[85]

The account of tanghin supplied in the anonymous *Beauties and Wonders of Vegetable Life* issued by the Religious Tract Society in 1866, was yet more lurid. If someone was judged guilty, but had not immediately died, the guilty party was bludgeoned, strangled, burnt or left to expire alone in excruciating agonies. Tanghin became an accessory to martyrdom: "Many Christian converts have been subjected to this cruel usage, and have proved faithful unto death."[86] In this evangelical re-telling, tanghin offered an exemplary tale of Christian fortitude under persecution.

Plant poisons were also associated with colonial warfare.[87] The Palm House displayed a number of spurges, including *Euphorbia grandidens*, notable for its poisonous sap. "The slightest incision in the bark," observed Hooker, "causes a great quantity of milky juice to flow, which, being of a highly acrid and venomous nature, is employed by the native Africans for poisoning their arrows and assagays."[88] Hooker's use of the term 'assegai' for spear evoked the weaponry of the Zulu and Xhosa people of southern Africa. The term would have been familiar to the British

85 Gosse (1857), 118-20.
86 *Beauties and Wonders of Vegetable Life; or Rambles in Parks, Forests, Conservatories, Orchards, Gardens, Fields and Heaths* (London: Religious Tracts Society, 1866), 121.
87 For poisoned arrows, see Simpson, D., "Poisonous arrows and unsound minds: hysterical tetanus in the Victorian South Pacific", in Dickson, M., Taylor-Brown, E., Shuttleworth, S., eds., *Progress and Pathology: Medicine and Culture in the Nineteenth Century* (Manchester: Manchester University Press, 2020), 269-91.
88 Hooker (1852), 26.

reading public from accounts of travel and military campaigns; throughout the nineteenth century, the British in the Cape Colony were engaged in successive wars against the Xhosa. The description of the sap of *Euphorbia grandidens* supplied in *Beauties and Wonders of Vegetable Life* heightened the violence implicit in Hooker's account: "it is a very strong poison in which the savage Africans dip their spears and arrows to make the wounds they inflict more dangerous to the lives of their foes."[89]

The most notorious arrow poison was *ipo*, made from the sap of the Javanese upas tree (*Antiaris toxicaria*). According to eighteenth-century European tales, the upas was so toxic that it blighted surrounding vegetation and littered the ground with the corpses of animals and birds. Michael Dove has argued that these accounts were co-produced by the Javanese themselves in a deliberate attempt to deter Europeans from venturing further inland and gaining control over valuable plant resources.[90] The upas featured in works by Byron, Pushkin, and the poet-naturalist Erasmus Darwin (grandfather of Charles Darwin), who termed it 'the Hydra Tree of death'. The term 'upas' even acquired the figurative meaning of deadly influence.[91] But, by the nineteenth century, the fabled tree had become the object of scientific investigation. The environmental devastation was thought to have been caused by the escape of carbonic acid gas (carbon dioxide) from the ground. The operation of *ipo* poison was tested through experiments on unfortunate dogs and cats. For Gosse, the upas provided the climax of his description of the Palm House display. Over several pages, he recounted stories of the plant's "terrible, though somewhat mythic celebrity," quoted at

89 *Beauties* [...] (1866), 121.

90 Dove, M. R., "Dangerous Plants in the Colonial Imagination: Rumphius and the Poison Tree", *Allertonia*, Vol. 13, 2014, 29-46.

91 For the upas, see Yule, H., A. C. Burnell, Teltscher K., ed., *Hobson-Jobson: The Definitive Glossary of British India* (Oxford: Oxford University Press, 2013), 533-40; Carey, D., "The political economy of poison: the kingdom of Makassar and the early Royal Society", *Renaissance Studies*, Vol. 17 No. 3, 2003, 517-543; Dove (2014); Hannigan, T., "Beyond control: Orientalist tensions and the history of the 'upas tree' myth", *The Journal of Commonwealth Literature*, Vol. 55 No. 2, 2020, 173-189.

length from Erasmus Darwin; then, in more scientific vein, itemised the ingredients and method for preparing *ipo*, and finally detailed its effects: trembling, loss of bowel control, spasms, convulsions, vomiting, agony and death.[92] While Gosse's account enacted the process of demystification from mythical horror to scientific precision, the upas emerged as no less deadly an agent of destruction.

The hazards posed by tropical vegetation were evidently part of the Palm House's appeal. An article in the *Quarterly Review* (1851) even included a plant that was no longer on display: "the most deadly plant ever possessed by Kew," *Jatropha urens* (*Cnidoscolus urens* or devil nettle). The plant had nearly cost the life of John Smith, the curator of Kew, the article related. "Some five and twenty years ago he was reaching over the *Jatropha*, when its fine bristly stings touched his wrist. The first sensation was a numbness and swelling of the lips; the action of the poison was on the heart, circulation was stopped, and Mr. Smith soon fell unconscious, the last thing he remembered being cries of 'Run for the doctor'."[93]

The narrative of John Smith's near-death experience was repeated in children's accounts of Kew issued by the popular religious press. *The Child's Companion and Juvenile Instructor* (1852), published by the Religious Tract Society, acknowledged that poison plants were difficult to reconcile with the divine scheme, but reassured readers that many of the operations of nature were beyond human comprehension. "We do not know the use of these poisonous qualities in plants, though we are quite certain that there is a reason why they are thus created, and that they are designed for some wise and good end."[94] The account of John Smith's collapse was also recycled as a cautionary tale by the *Monthly Packet of Evening Readings for Younger Members of the Church of England* (1854).

92 Gosse (1857), 139-43.
93 *Quarterly Review* 179 (1851), 48.
94 *Child's Companion and Juvenile Instructor* (1852), 52.

Children who visited the Palm House were enjoined to pay "due attention to the placards, entreating visitors not to touch the plants, for there have been in this collection, and perchance may be again, specimens of the most deadly and poisonous plants."[95]

While the religious press sought to moralise the Palm House display, secular accounts emphasised its popular appeal. By the 1870s, enhanced railway links caused an explosion in visitor numbers to Kew (one summer day in 1870, the turnstile registered 33,000 visitors). With crowds such as these, commentators questioned the educational benefits of a visit to Kew. In 1871, Henry Walker asserted that, for the masses, "these vegetable captives from mysterious countries afar off are as fearful and wonderful as the tigers and giraffes in the Zoological Gardens." According to Walker, "Kew Gardens happily provide for all variety of tastes and grades of capacity. They are a promenade for the fashionable, a museum for the student, as well as a thrilling picture of vegetable monsters and curiosities to the sight-seeing holiday-maker."[96] With the zoological parallel and visitor categorisation, Walker anticipated the arguments of environmental historian, Harriet Ritvo. For Ritvo, Kew resembled London's Zoological Gardens in "its complex presentation of wild nature and human control, as well as its simultaneous appeal to the scientific, technical and popular constituencies."[97] As Ritvo has argued, both institutions attempted to combine scientific display with public education and mass entertainment. At Kew, these aims coalesced around the plant houses, in particular the central attraction, the Palm House. A visit to Kew offered nineteenth-century Londoners a thrilling encounter with tropical beauty, danger and violence. The increasing popularity of Kew as a visitor destination turned the Palm House into a spectacle.

95 *Monthly Packet of Evening Readings* 46 (October 1854), 309.

96 Walker, H., *Saturday Afternoon Rambles round London* (London: Hodder and Stoughton, 1871), 113.

97 Ritvo, H., "The Natural World" in Mackenzie, J., ed., *The Victorian Vision: Inventing New Britain* (London: V&A Publications, 2001), 287.

The specimens on display were accompanied by colonial and missionary narratives that emphasised the deadly properties of plants. If the plants themselves were not endowed with murderous intent, as in fictional planthorror, they certainly possessed the capacity to injure and kill. In 1873 the *Edinburgh Review* memorably described the Palm House as a "prison house... for the captured forest trees of the tropics."[98] As this essay has demonstrated, the popular journalism and literature of the nineteenth-century Palm House provided fertile ground for the subsequent development of plant horror. In 1900, an article in the *Daily News* reported on "the poorer visitors" as they wandered through "the show places" of Kew. In the Palm House, "there was much fun on the spiral staircase." One courting couple was particularly observed:

> "Any of them man-eating plants here?" asked a girl, evidently given to the reading of magazine tales. "Of course," replied her companion, "and if they don't grab you at once they run after you." The young lady told him to "Go on," but she was evidently a little nervous.[99]

98 *Edinburgh Review* (1873), 266.
99 *Daily News* (August 20th, 1900), 6.

Telling Stories with Plant Cases

an essay by Adriana Craciun

One way of telling the story of Wardian plant cases as colonial technologies is Australian historian and curator Luke Keogh's approach in *The Wardian Case: How a Simple Box Moved Plants and Changed the World* (2020).[100] This story begins with the invention of the technology in Britain and follows its imperial travels to and from metropole and peripheries, with Kew Gardens at the heart of the narrative. Building on the glazed plant boxes used aboard eighteenth-century long-distance voyages like that of French naval officer Comte de La Pérouse, English doctor and plant enthusiast Nathaniel Bagshaw Ward developed his own model in 1829 that hereafter associated his name with this proxy technology for European scientific imperialism.[101] As befitting a book published in collaboration with Kew, Keogh's story reinforces nineteenth-century Eurocentric models of heroic technology, and of metropolitan powers vs passive colonies – boxes moving plants and changing the world. This story also follows the 'fatal impact' narrative that in recent decades has been questioned in postcolonial anthropology, history, and geography in favour of more nuanced attention to the specificity of Indigenous/European encounters, and the agency of Indigenous people before and beyond contact.

Boxes do not move plants – currents, winds, ice, continents, and animals move plants. And, of course, plants move themselves across immense

100 Keogh, L., *The Wardian Case: How a Simple Box Moved Plants and Changed the World* (Chicago: University of Chicago Press/Kew Publishing, 2020).

101 On La Pérouse's plant cases, see Destouff Milet-Mureau, L., ed., *Voyage de La Pérouse autour du monde*, Vol. 1, (Paris: de l'Imprimerie de la République, 1797), 212.

distances in time and space through ingenious contrivances like seed dispersal. Ward himself acknowledged that his "closed cases are as old as creation," because in the polar regions, "the snow itself affords shelter to the productions of those inhospitable regions against the piercing winds that sweep over the fields of everlasting ice. Under the cold defence of the snow, plants spring up and dissolve the snow a few inches round. The part above being again quickly frozen into a transparent sheet of ice, admits the sun's rays which warm and cherish the plant in this natural hothouse."[102] Many Arctic and Alpine plants have indeed developed this ability to shelter inside 'natural hothouses' beneath the ice, so that as Ward recognised, the story of closed cases and greenhouses might begin with the lives of plants themselves.

In order to decolonise the Wardian case, we need to begin our stories elsewhere and elsewhen: not with Ward's biography or his invention, or the institutions like Kew that employed them, but with the ecological and cultural exchanges at the turn of the nineteenth century and long before, across beaches, islands, and ice that accelerated the travels of plants globally. Take the iconic plant exemplifying European colonial plant transfer – breadfruit (*Artocarpus*) – which was transplanted aboard British ships at the turn of the nineteenth century from Tahiti to Caribbean colonies to serve as cheap food for enslaved labourers. In important works on the imbrication of European plant transfer, empire, and the slave trade, professors Alan Bewell and Elizabeth Deloughrey have independently depicted Captain William Bligh's 1793 voyage transporting "Tahitian food trees" as a "historical event" initiating the "globalisation of the island tropics" through plant transfer.[103] But like many other Tahitian plants that Europeans would collect and recirculate using their ships and plant cases, breadfruit were

102 Bagshaw Ward, N., *On the Growth of Plants in Closely Glazed Cases* (London: John Van Voorst, 1842), 67.
103 DeLoughrey, E., "Globalizing the Routes of Breadfruit and Other Bounties," in *Journal of Colonialism and Colonial History* 8 (2007); see also Bewell, A., *Natures in Translation: Romanticism and Colonial Natural Histories* (Baltimore: Johns Hopkins University Press, 2017), 96-100.

not native to Tahiti, and Europeans did not initiate their global movements. Breadfruit were among the many species of desirable plants (and animals) that Polynesians transplanted long distances on their voyages as they settled the vast Pacific basin over a thousand years before Europeans arrived.[104]

The Lapita ancestors of modern Polynesians sailed with living plants protected in an ingenious range of devices, some swinging from the roof of the huts of their double-hulled canoes,[105] travelling thousands of miles and reaching islands where they transplanted and acclimatised their desired flora. Thousands of years ago, the Lapita "transported and established the biotic and cultural components necessary to re-create in each new island precisely the kind of managed landscape they had just left behind."[106] The Lapita are known by their distinctively ornate ceramic vessels which served both practical and spiritual roles, and "may have been essential to colonising groups while their horticultural systems were being established."[107] The plants and animals travelling in their oceangoing vessels irreversibly affected the ecosystems of the islands they settled; combined with the use of fire and intensive horticulture, and the resulting erosion and deforestation, these transplants resulted in the extirpation of dozens of indigenous plant, bird, and mammal species across the diverse ecosystems of Oceania, before European contact.

These long-distance voyages of transplantation were thought (by European historians) to have been accidental, but are now understood to have been deliberate exploratory and colonising voyages, as Oceanic accounts

104 For a detailed study see Cox, P. A. and Banack, S. A., eds, *Islands, Plants, and Polynesians: An Introduction to Polynesian Ethnobotany* (Portland: Dioscorides Press, 1991).

105 Bevacqua, R., "Origin of Horticulture in Southeast Asia and the Dispersal of Domesticated Plants to the Pacific Islands by Polynesian Voyagers", in *Horticultural Science*, Vol. 29 No. 11, (1994), 1228. Alison Atkins offers a detailed study in her MS dissertation on *An Experiment in the Transportation of Culturally Significant Plant Propagules on Polynesian Voyaging Canoes* (Honolulu: University of Hawai'i, 2013), 24-38.

106 Kirch, P. V., *On the Road of the Winds: An Archaeological History of the Pacific Islands Before European Contact* (Berkeley: University of California Press, 2017), 109.

107 Kirch (2017), 106.

have long held. For example, Maori oral accounts tell of the *Hakirere waka* (ocean-going canoe) that set out on a long voyage to collect and return desirable plants: "The Nga Rauru and Ngati Ruanui ancestor Maru came across the taro plant growing on a distant island while exploring on the Moana-nui-a-Kiwa. Upon returning home, he showed his people this new plant and induced them to return to the island Wairuangangana... to procure roots of the plant for cultivation. In due course two waka... set out to retrace Maru's course," and successfully brought taro and *kumara* (sweet potato) which were then cultivated in Maori gardens.[108] Such Polynesian plant transfer and cultivation across the vast Pacific produced "massive ecosystem disturbances," which remain inseparable from the extraordinary "exploits of fishers who domesticated an important assemblage of tropical plants, [and] the daring Polynesian navigators who dispersed them over a sizeable portion of the globe (long before Europeans were sailing out of sight of land)."[109]

Aboard British explorer James Cook's global voyages of the 1760s and 1770s were the first Europeans to begin to glimpse this extraordinary transoceanic network of cultivated island communities, sharing languages, plants, and cultural connections across distances that dwarfed those of maritime European empires. Johann Reinhold Forster, a German naturalist on Cook's first circumnavigation, understood that many Oceanic plants were those which "the first settlers of these isles brought with them from their original East-Indian seats," and that they had been "improved" into numerous new seedless varieties propagated by Polynesian horticulturalists.[110] As the scale of this Oceanic network of plants, people, and culture became clearer, Cook marveled how "it is extraordinary that the same Nation should have spread themselves over all the isles

108 Evans, J., *Nga Waka o Nehera: The First Voyaging Canoes* (1997; Auckland: Libro International, 2009), 49.
109 Bevacqua (1994), 1228-9.
110 Forster, J., *Observations Made During a Voyage Round the World*, edited by Thomas, N., Guest, H., and Dettelbach, M., (Honolulu: University of Hawai'i Press, 1996), 120.

of this vast ocean... which is almost one-fourth part of the circumference of the globe."[111] If we tell the story of plant cases within this larger story of oceanic plant transfer, where European routes criss-cross much older and more elaborate routes of plant transfer via Polynesian ocean-going vessels and their shipboard technologies, then we can tell new stories about these vessels of meaning that do not star Europeans as the prime movers.

All objects come bearing multiple stories, and Ward's plant case as a technology of colonial conquest is only one. Ward envisioned his plant case as a means of transporting plants to people and vice versa – a vessel with as much local value as the global role emphasised in imperial studies. The inner-city poor and invalids were the immediate beneficiaries and customers, as Ward saw it, of plant transfer from the local countryside, with native plants providing an aesthetic, medicinal, and spiritual benefit on the window thresholds of the human homes they shared. Wood sorrel, primroses, ivy, and other local flora transplanted from the outskirts of London would do well in cases in inner London according to Ward, and growing radishes or lettuce along with the wild plants could supplement the diets of the poor.[112] Those suffering from consumption or measles, instead of going "to a distant land for a remote chance at recovery," could convalesce in a large "closed house" with an atmosphere purified by plants.[113] Like conservatories, greenhouses, exhibition spaces, winter gardens, and arcades, Wardian cases were part of the new urban "glass fantasia" that British academic Isobel Armstrong has explored in her book, *Victorian Glassworlds: Glass Culture and the Imagination 1830-1880*[114] – heterogeneous spaces in every sense, populated by plants and people of bewildering varieties.

111 Cook, J., *A Voyage Towards the South Pole and Round the World*, Vol. 1, (London: W. Strahan and T. Cadell, 1777), 290.
112 Bagshaw Ward (1842), 93.
113 Bagshaw Ward (1842), 112. Shirley Hibberd also recommends the therapeutic effects of plant cases in *Rustic Adornments for Homes of Taste* (London: Groombridge and Sons, 1856), 135-8.
114 (Oxford: Oxford University Press, 2008).

Wardian cases also fueled the nineteenth-century fern craze (also referred to as *pteridomania*) that introduced into domestic spaces plants from distant colonies across oceans, and into urban spaces ferns from across the British isles. These same fern cases (ferneries) allowed the creation of simulacra of lost ecosystems of the Carboniferous Period, microcosms of a plant-dominated planet long before humans became part of Earth's stories. In *British and Garden Botany* (1864), the English botanist Leopold Hartley Grindon described how gazing at ferns transports "one to the Age of Ferns, when the world was a kind of enormous Wardian case, and the advent of man was still far in the distant future."[115] Israeli researcher Naomi Yuval-Naeh argues that this proliferation of *pteridomania* through Wardian cases made the case a "complex symbolic carrier of the preindustrial world, and at the same time, of the origin of all industries, a Carboniferous forest properly domesticated and miniaturized to fit the parlour."[116] In allowing nineteenth-century fern enthusiasts to create their fantasies of a Carboniferous forest, the source of the coal driving the age of industry, Wardian cases and their "climate within a climate"[117] activated a "power to transport their viewers across time and to enable them literally to touch a relic of the distant past."[118] But ultimately it was the plants and their ecosystems that moved people through time, not the other way around, and not the boxes.

Decentering humans as the protagonists of Earth's histories, transforming urban natures (as a tool of social engineering, in the moral "improvement" of the poor), and serving as a therapeutic interface with plant worlds, are some of the popular dimensions of Wardian cases that we need to reconnect to their equally important imperial dimensions.

115 Grindon, L. H., *British and Garden Botany* (London: Routledge, 1864), 800. I am grateful to Yuval-Naeh's essay for drawing my attention to this work.

116 Yuval-Naeh, N., "Cultivating the Carboniferous: Coal as a Botanical Curiosity in Victorian Culture", in *Victorian Studies*, Vol. 61 No. 3, (2019), 419-45.

117 Hibberd (1856), 127.

118 Yuval-Naeh (2019), 440.

And as an iteration of much older technologies of plant transfer, crossing oceans outside the influence of European empires, plant cases share with Polynesian vessels unpredictable possibilities of mobility. To decolonise objects like plant cases, we have to attend to their complex genealogies across cultures and trace the polycentric spaces they travel throughout their varied social lives, enlivened by plants.

Gardening at Home: Liberating Middle-class Women in 19th-century Britain

an essay by Penny Sparke

The era of industrialisation in Britain saw many people move from rural areas to cities, severing their longstanding links with the countryside and the natural world. To fill that gap in their lives, the new urban dwellers began to bring nature, in the form of plants and flowers, into their homes. Industrialisation also created a new gendered division of labour in middle-class households: While men earned money outside the home, women stayed inside it, nurturing their children, and creating a safe and beautiful haven for the family. That latter role included taking on the responsibility for the decoration of the home, which included displaying the new plants and flowers that were entering it for the first time. As a result, women quickly developed a special relationship with their indoor greenery. That special relationship between women and, what had long been referred to as, 'Mother Nature' was not new, however. It simply extended to the nature indoors as well as outdoors. The gendered division of labour – often called 'The Separate Spheres' – simply reinforced that longstanding alliance.

As many of the plants and flowers that were brought into houses were homegrown, they required the protection of the heated spaces in greenhouses. By the eighteenth century, many wealthy landowners had constructed greenhouses in their private walled gardens. A century later the urban middle classes were emulating them and building their own greenhouses in their smaller back gardens. The numerous exotic plants – rubber plants and cacti among them – that were so popular at the time, and which added a touch of class to otherwise modest interiors, also benefited from being enclosed in the glazed greenhouses and in the conservatories which began to be attached to urban and suburban homes. The fashion for domestic conservatories grew as middle-class families emulated the owners of large country houses who had created enclosed spaces near their houses in which they could not only grow exotic plants but into which they could also invite visitors to take tea and stroll among the plants. In 1876 Joseph Paxton launched a conservatory kit, advertised as "glasshouses for the million," helping to further extend the market for domestic conservatories in the urban setting even further. The domestication, and accompanying feminisation, of the conservatory attached to the home transformed it from an object of scientific interest into a cultural artefact with aesthetic and symbolic value.

Views differed about whether conservatories being attached to the house was a good thing. While the landscape gardener, Humphry Repton, advocated attaching them to lighten up the parlour he also advised the inclusion of a small passageway between the parlour and the conservatory to avoid unpleasant smells – such as rotting earth – travelling from the latter to the former. John Claudius Loudon, another of the nineteenth century's best-known gardening experts, on the other hand, felt that the smell of flowers wafting into the house was a definite benefit. Some writers from the period encouraged the addition of fish, sculpture, and seats in domestic conservatories to create environments in which afternoon tea could be enjoyed and proposals of marriage made.

The greenhouse and the conservatory took on different gendered meanings. As Henry T. Williams, an American author of a window gardening advice book explained, "The one [the conservatory] is mainly devoted to ornamental purposes, and the exhibition of plants in full beauty of growth and bloom, while in the humbler greenhouse, propagating boxes are the chief furniture used by the gardener for the production and forcing of his young plants." While, traditionally, the greenhouse had been linked with practical masculine work, the conservatory was associated with decorative feminine activities. As urban women began to enter their domestic greenhouses, however, the boundary between that strict division began to become blurred.

To display the plants and flowers that entered the house itself, a range of indoor plant and flower containers – terraria, Wardian cases and enclosed window gardens among them – began to appear in already cluttered Victorian parlours. Advice book writers – from (James) Shirley Hibberd to John R. Mollison – wrote at length about them. In his *Rustic Adornments for Homes of Taste* of 1856 the former dedicated large sections of his text to the construction of indoor fern cases; combined fern cases and aquaria; and enclosed window gardens, while also advising amateur (for which read 'female') gardeners on the best way to propagate plants in the greenhouse.

Working with the plants and flowers that filled their greenhouses, conservatories and indoor living spaces had a liberating effect on women. While, to undertake their other domestic 'accomplishments' – including embroidery, knitting, shell-work, hair-work, leather-work, work with moss and pine cones, wool work and crochet – they had to remain in their homes, greenhouses allowed them to leave the four walls of the house. Attached conservatories enabled them to be both inside and outside at the same time while remaining protected from the harsh effects of bad weather. They were also liberated by the fact that their new responsibilities extended to not only arranging plants and flowers in decorative settings but also to taking over from men much of the work involved in growing them.

Some of the evidence that that sense of liberation was real (or was at least perceived to be real), and that working with plants brought women a great deal of pleasure, satisfaction, independence, and confidence in their new self-identities, can be found in the pages of the outdoor and indoor gardening advice books, several of them written by women, that were published through the middle years of the nineteenth century.

Advice books played an important role in encouraging women to undertake such work and giving them useful tips. The first ones were written about women embracing outdoor gardening. Starting with the work of Jane Wells Webb Loudon – including *Gardening for Ladies* of 1843, *The Ladies' Country Companion* of 1845, *The Ladies' Flower Garden of Ornamental Greenhouse Plants* of 1848 and *The Ladies' Companion to the Flower Garden* of 1858 – women had been encouraged to engage in horticulture. That moved, in the urban setting, to window gardening and to women's desire to grow their own plants and flowers for indoor settings.

Although very few women engaged in professional horticulture at that time, some exceptions to that rule emerged in the second half of the century. They included Lady Dorothy Nevill who turned the estate garden at her large Sussex property, 'Dangstein' near Petersfield, acquired in 1851, into a horticultural landmark, with seventeen conservatories housing her exotic plants. She went on to supply Charles Darwin with rare plants for his research. Women such as Lady Nevill acted as role models for middle-class women who sought to go beyond arranging flowers in a vase and engage with the science of horticulture.

One indoor gardening advice book, *Every Lady's Guide to her own Greenhouse, Hothouse, and Conservatory: Instructions for Cultivating Plants which Require Protection* of 1851, which was written by an anonymous 'Lady', explained how much women enjoyed working with plants. This was partly due, the author explained, to the widespread belief that nature was made by God himself (which was thought to please women), as well as to the conviction that seeing fragile plants and flowers flourish made women happy. The fact that that sense of happiness also derived from looking after plants by oneself, rather than requiring help from anyone else, was also seen as an important step forward in women's newfound self-reliance. Nurturing plants also staved off boredom, the Lady explained, and some writers went as far as to claim that tamed plants provided otherwise lonely women with companionship.

The advice books also claimed that women derived much satisfaction from acquiring horticultural skills and seeing through a complete process – from, that is, sowing seeds to placing a potted plant on an indoor table. Above all, it was felt that women could follow their own whims and desires when they worked in an urban greenhouse as they were no longer being told by a skilled male gardener that they were doing things wrong. There was still a widespread acknowledgement, however, that, when it came to lifting heavy things, women needed some help from a male servant, but that he should follow her instructions and because he lacked horticultural skills, he was not able to tell her what to do. This was clearly, the advice books tell us, a new, liberating, and much appreciated, experience for many women. In her book, the Lady included a long section on constructing a greenhouse. Although she would undoubtedly have had help from a man to make it, she provided very detailed technical specifications, thereby indicating a very close involvement with that building project. In taking on the whole process of growing and nurturing plants to displaying them in their indoor settings women were engaging with both science and art. Artistic activities – including the 'accomplishments' listed above and the interior decoration of the home – were seen to come 'naturally' to them. However, potting, planting cuttings, and sowing seeds, which took place in greenhouses and required some horticultural expertise, were not. Middle-class women acquired that expertise through personal experience and perseverance, rather than through formal training or education (from which they were excluded for the most part at that time).

In her 1862 book, *Indoor Plants, and How to Grow Them, for the Drawing Room, Balcony and Greenhouse*, Miss E. A. Maling pointed out that more urban than rural women were taking over from men, claiming that skilled gardeners were still employed in the latter. That was undoubtedly the case as large country houses still employed teams of gardeners led by head gardeners. The head gardener's role extended as far as selecting the flowers that were given to the lady of the house to make floral arrangements for the dining table. As Miss Maling observed, in the city many women were undertaking potting, planting cuttings, and sowing seeds as well as bringing the fruits of their labours inside. This was largely due to the absence of skilled employees, (whether by choice or economic expediency). Her text was rooted in the assumption that being able to grow their own plants and flowers for their homes was both very satisfying and pleasurable for women. Among many other subjects, she discussed conservatories, miniature greenhouses, Waltonian cases, how to plant cuttings, how to winter plants, and how to make a heated plant stand from an old oak coffee table. She also went as far as suggesting the kind of tiles to use on a conservatory floor, and how women could transfer to their flowers their knowledge about colour acquired in the context of their dress.

The fact that urban women were being encouraged by advice books to combine some light scientific practices with artistic work in the home redefined feminine work, taking it beyond the conventional duties expected of the 'Angel of the House' as defined by 'The Separate Spheres'. As a consequence, many middle-class women began to re-assess their own self-identities and to challenge the ideology that had restricted them to decorative work in the home. Nurturing was included, but of children, not plants and flowers. No longer simply at the service of the men of the house, women became increasingly independent. They began to teach themselves some horticulture, enjoy getting their hands dirty in the greenhouse and conservatory, and appreciate the pleasures and sense of satisfaction that could be found there. Arguably, the potential for liberation that was offered to middle-class women by the arrival of urban greenhouses and conservatories aligned with the many other ways in which, by the end of the nineteenth century, they had begun to question their designated role and to demand equal rights to those of men.

III. Current Stories

From strawberries and cherry tomatoes to roses and cucumbers, numerous are the plants at the heart of the contemporary monocultural and intensive agricultural system. The greenhouses that host such productions are the theatres of many social, ethical and environmental issues. By looking at the controversies of three specific contexts, the interviews presented here aim at revealing some of the questions that these modern production tools bring about.

The Cut Flower Industry: from Kenya to Scotland

d-o-t-s in conversation with Natalya Ayers, Fiona Inglis and Coltrane McDowell[119]
photos by Coltrane McDowell

What lies behind a bouquet of roses? Is a rose still a rose when it has grown under a vast greenhouse, disconnected from other plants and insects? What does it mean to work against the globalised flow of horticultural production? This conversation with flower designers and growers Natalya Ayers and Fiona Inglis, and with Canadian designer Coltrane McDowell analyses critically the cut-flower industry and discusses how flowers can change the world.

d-o-t-s As you all share a militant and creative passion for flowers, we thought it would be nice to start our conversation with a provocation borrowed from the title of an installation of French artist, Camille Henrot: *Is it possible to Be a Revolutionary and Like Flowers?*

Fiona Inglis Yes, definitely! I think flowers would inspire any revolutionary with their quiet determination. It takes a lot of energy for growing, blossoming and creating change, which is what being a revolutionary is.

Natalya Ayers I agree. To me, the term revolutionary applies to someone who wants to change the system, or make something new. I believe that gardening can definitely be a political statement and a way to participate in changing society. Growing and reconnecting with Nature is quite anti-global and anti-commercialisation.

119 Zoom conversation recorded by d-o-t-s on November 20th, 2021.

There is an essay by the American writer Rebecca Solnit that I find very inspiring in that sense: it is titled *Revolutionary Plots* (2012)[120] and in it, Solnit talks about gardens as refuges or interventions.

Coltrane McDowell At the same time, I wonder if flowers represent some kind of establishment too? If you look at the recent COVID-19 pandemic, for instance, flowers seem to have embodied the controversies of all the industries linked, nowadays, to just-in-time delivery and hyper-globalised-on-demand lifestyle – somehow they became symbols of the status quo. On the other hand, it is true that flowers can also be used as a means to challenge that establishment and ask: "Do we want these ways of living to continue in the next years or decades?"

d-o-t-s Yes, one might say that flowers have a double identity. Especially if you think about how the history of the cut flower industry is profoundly linked to practices such as genetic selection, monocultural production and pesticides. As creatives who work with flowers' fragility and ephemerality, how do you feel about this 'heritage' and the effects it has on the way we perceive and 'consume' flowers in Western society? What are the dangers of reducing flowers to commodities?

NA For me, and in our work at Pyrus, the fragility of the flowers and their transience has always been something that we embraced and were attracted by. It is almost the very essence of our work. You are following something's life cycle and that can be so fragile. Fiona and I have always used every part of a plant: from the flowers and petals to the seeds and roots, but also the soil that it grows in and sometimes even compost or ash from the bonfire... This life cycle is important, and I think that that is what is being lost when flowers are reduced to commodities. We are disconnected

120 ◊ www.orionmagazine.org/article/revolutionary-plots.

from them. For so many years we have been shown only mass-produced, homogenised and perfect flowers that one can consume easily and cheaply, without truly appreciating them.

FI I think that what makes me uncomfortable is the scale and the ideal proposed by monocultures. It sort of all comes back to that sense of disconnection Natalya mentioned: monocultural production results in identical flowers with no personality nor character of their own; they are not precious and people cannot connect with them anymore.

d-o-t-s A powerful example of disconnection created by monocultures is the loss of scent in flowers that are cultivated primarily for the beauty of their blossoms. Roses are a good example in that regard.

NA To me it seems nonsensical to breed the scent out of a rose so that it lasts longer. The scent is what makes a rose a rose, it is so intoxicating and evocative. When one thinks that whole generations – particularly in cities, where people can't necessarily afford a garden – have grown up only knowing commercially grown roses without scent, that is incredibly sad.

CM You are right, Natalya, many people never experience the scent of a real rose! Most of the flower production that happens in Kenya, for instance, focuses on unscented roses. The farm that I was on was quite an anomaly as they produce roses specifically for their scents.

FI It doesn't make any sense and there is also some kind of deeper connection with the seasons that is lost with that. That's what I have learnt from growing our own: how being in tune with the seasons is really something intrinsic to us, as natural beings.

And I think that's another harmful element from that detachment from flowers: people lose that understanding and that connection with the seasons and therefore lose a little bit of understanding in themselves too. We really live in a world that is cut off from Nature.

NA I actually wonder if flowers grown in vast greenhouses are still themselves? We are now aware of how important fungi and microorganisms present in the soil are; how trees can effectively 'talk' to each other thanks to mycorrhizal networks; and how all the plants are connected in their community. Can we really consider flowers that are grown in big commercial greenhouses – sometimes with no soil at all, as that can be more efficient – as real flowers? There is so much lacking in these flowers that they can't possibly bring the same amount of joy or knowledge or history. The primal instinct of a plant to seed and sprout – it simply doesn't exist. They haven't got that much to give because they don't have that quality themselves, they are soulless.

d-o-t-s Going back to the notion of fragility, Coltrane, you developed your research at a critical moment for the global cut flower industry, in the spring of 2020, when COVID-19 hit for the first time and flights connecting Kenya (one of the main producers of roses globally) to Europe were grounded...

CM Yes, the cut flower industry is an important segment of Kenya's economy. The number of people that are tied to a single rose's life cycle and potential sale is greater than the rose itself. So when the pandemic happened, the farm that I was working on – which would have had 100 people working on-site on a regular basis – was down to 10. This really had an impact on the flower sector locally. So in regard to the notion of fragility, I think the main fragility here lies in the economic system itself.

d-o-t-s The key element of your project was the use of wasted roses to produce a new product – a rose scent – that could help diversify the local industry and provide additional income, especially in these difficult times. What kind of reaction did your project generate?

CM There was the intention within the rose farming community to go into essential oil production. I was working with alcohol distillers in Nairobi and there was a real desire from the local low-income people to engage in the sector. Since then, I received a couple of requests, primarily from perfumers looking for ethically sourced fragrant materials. A company called Black Perfumers, for example, wanted to source African-owned products that directly benefitted communities. So yes, there is an interest and this is exciting, but even if you have an idea there are many challenges in Kenya when you are working within the flower industry and with low-income communities: there is a lot of corruption and the market is dominated by people who want to keep it a certain way and aren't interested in diversifying the economy. Also, the essential oil industry is heavily dominated by Europe and is quite colonial in its structure. The processes that are used to extract these scents are questionable too. If there were real changes to happen they would have to be initiated from The Netherlands which is the main buyer for these flowers and sets standards that all growers must respect.

d-o-t-s Can you tell us more about the production of roses in Kenya?

CM A lot of the rose production happens where there is a steady supply of water and also at a certain altitude where you can grow all year round. There are essentially no seasons and you have a continuous production cycle. There have always been questions around the sustainability of flower farms because they need large quantities of water and, of course, when you are using water for one thing, you are diverting it from other people and industries, but also from the environment. Water is a big issue: in terms of extraction but also in terms of treatment. For instance, the wastewater that comes out of the farms in Naivasha – which is the main industrialised agricultural flower farming area in Kenya – runs directly into Lake Naivasha. And even in the farm that I was working in – which is quite advanced in regard to ethical standards – they would still spray their crops with a heavy amount of pesticides every day.

NA I wonder, what is it like in those closed environments in regard to pollinators and other insects?

CM In the greenhouses, there is basically nothing. Maybe a couple of flies, but you really don't see much. It is a rather sterile environment compared to the rich wildlife around the farms. Flowers are grown semi indoor in greenhouses with shadings and small openings, so they are not completely hermetic spaces. As Kenya has a year-round temperate climate, the shadings are actually used to protect the roses from the sun, which could damage them or prevent them from growing homogeneously.

d-o-t-s Fiona and Natalya, as advocates of the Slow Flower Movement, what is your point of view on the global flower market, especially in light of the recent events? How did the pandemic impact you as small growers? Was it the occasion for you to tell a different story from the one that was seen in the media – where imported flowers were dumped in the thousands, for instance?

FI We experienced an interesting reaction here in how the pandemic affected our business. With the lockdown, all events such as weddings were cancelled and flower shops were closed. All that chain came to a stop. In the beginning, it was difficult and we wondered if anybody would actually want flowers. But the answer was that people very much did! It was the first time we had a subscription service set up and it really brought things back to the core of what I had originally loved about flowers: the way they can communicate. While delivering flowers to people, you would see the complete joy that they brought: for people who couldn't see their loved ones, the simple gesture of offering flowers was making such a big difference.

NA It was really sad to see so many flowers thrown away. I remember thinking: can't they do something else with them? Aren't there initiatives to compost them or use them for natural dyes? The pandemic highlighted so many holes in the global flower industry. It has shown that it is urgent to readdress it all. With the Slow Flower Movement blossoming all over the US and Europe, I think this is an opportunity to say: "Here are all the things that they have done wrong."

CM I agree with you, the pandemic highlighted the fact that the entire system is unsustainable and so, of course, this drive towards locally sourced and locally produced flowers is the perfect initiative. But then I wonder about all the other countries that have been dragged into the system. The Netherlands gains a lot from having poorer countries produce what they then sell at a higher export price. Because they are just the auction house, they have no responsibility for any of the people working in the flower farms. So when you have countries such as Colombia or Kenya – where the flower industry is one of the main sectors providing employment – what could be the new alternative if we are going into these hyper sustainable/local models? I think that if we are looking after ourselves, we will have to think of how other countries can be self-sustaining as well.

NA The flower demand is so big – in terms of events and weddings especially – that I am not sure the Slow Flower production supply would be sufficient everywhere anyway. Obviously, I like local flowers, slow farms and the seasonality they imply, but I am not against flowers being produced in Kenya, if that can be done ethically and in an environmentally-safe way. The industries in Kenya, Colombia and Ecuador, for instance, are particularly important for women. So I don't condemn them completely, but I do think things need to be readdressed.

FI That's what is particularly interesting about your project, Coltrane: that idea of diversification and having multiple uses for a crop. On a small scale, this is something we have been aware of: that one plant may have multiple uses. So we grow willow for our own designs, but it can also be sold to weavers; the apples will go in our designs too but some will be harvested to make apple vinegar, and so on. Here our pick season is from April to October. In between, there are very few flowers available. So, exploring the idea of diversification and how this can be balanced with seasonality in other parts of the world is interesting.

CM How can creatives engage in these sorts of systems? I think it is interesting to question what is beautiful about a flower. As you said, Natalya and Fiona, you are using all the components of the flowers. It is not just the actual bloom that is beautiful, but all the other components. In a way, it is showing people that other aspects of the flower industry are beautiful. If everyone desires a 100-rose set, that is not very sustainable, but, if they want diversification, maybe it can be one rose from Ecuador mixed with a bunch of other locally produced seasonal plants.

FI Yes and yet, there is still a lot of education to be done to teach people about seasonality. Recently, I was speaking to somebody who wanted to do a photoshoot in mid-December and kept asking me "what flowers are there?" I said to the person: "Well, there aren't any, but there are all these beautiful textures and movements." In general, people aren't tuned in to that — they simply don't know. It is not always possible to be 100% 'green' if someone is getting married in the depth of winter. There are very few people who are happy with mosses and dried things. Most people expect to have a flowery event. That's why I think these conversations are really important.

d-o-t-s But so, in the end, shouldn't the revolution start from changing the consumers' behaviours and tastes? It is true that a lot of people don't know where the flowers they buy come from and how they were produced. Are you aware of initiatives that help consumers identify a flower's story (as it is now done widely with food)? Do you know of any labelling systems already implemented, for example?

FI At the end of 2020, an initiative was launched by the Scottish government to support a group that is now called Flowers Grown in Scotland. It is a collective of different growers from all over the country with different skills. The group's goal is to build awareness of Scottish flowers and also to identify ways to grow the sector to overcome the issues that are in place. I think that the environmental issues that go along with this industry are immense. So it is really important that money and support are put into these smaller groups to help them grow and provide a more environmental alternative to the big system that sees flowers travelling halfway across the world. One of the things that Flowers Grown in Scotland has been working on is the labelling. So we have a logo, everyone that joins the group is issued with stickers and the stickers are used on flowers that are solely growing in Scotland. But it takes time for that to become recognised and to get into circulation. I think something like that would be very beneficial with imported flowers too. Coltrane, you said the farm you worked at had some ethical regulations in place. Do they have some labelling system in place? As a florist, I know that this is something I would look for and I know that other professionals from this industry would too. People want to make informed choices.

CM Yes, they have their accreditations on their websites and through the companies that distribute their flowers in The Netherlands and in the UK. These accreditations are quite advantageous as people want to buy more of their products because they guarantee that the flowers meet certain standards.

NA Most florists buy from Holland, and often you would do that through online auctions. Wouldn't it be great if Royal FloraHolland and those auction sites had a 'Conscious' section with all the growers who are trying to grow in a more respectful manner, even though it isn't perfect? As a florist, I would certainly go straight to that section to see what I could get from there!

Mar de Plástico. Europe's Vegetable Garden

Téa Laurent in conversation with Joanna Moreno Michels [121]
photos by Simon Lenskens

"When viewed from a satellite, the expanse of greenhouses in Almería resembles a monochromatic patchwork quilt, stitched together by roads," [122] described landscape architect Melissa Cate Christ back in 2013 in a review detailing the critical environmental situation of the region known as Mar de plástico, in the south of Spain. Report after report, documentary after documentary, article after article, have things changed under the Spanish sun? French designer Téa Laurent discusses the issue with Almería-based journalist and syndicalist Joanna Moreno Michels.

Téa Laurent The agricultural production under greenhouses in the region of Almería is considered an 'economic miracle' and a promising model, especially when it comes to water consumption. So much so that some foreign states – such as California, in the USA – are currently studying ways to replicate it. How do you feel about this 'model'? [123]

Joanna Moreno Michels To be honest, when you know the reality, considering the region of Almería as a 'promising model' is enough to make people laugh. What are those defending this model really thinking?

121 Conversation originally in French, recorded by Téa Laurent on November 25th, 2021.
122 Christ, M. K., *This Garden of the Sun: A Report on Almería's Miracle Economy* (2013). ◊ www.scapegoatjournal.org/docs/05/SG_Excess_364-371_P_CateChrist.pdf (Accessed: January 15th, 2021).
123 To learn more about the working conditions behind Mar de plàstico's 'model', see Rippingale, J., "Consumers are not aware we are slaves inside the greenhouses", *Aljazeera online*, October 16th, 2019. ◊ www.aljazeera.com/features/2019/10/16/consumers-are-not-aware-we-are-slaves-inside-the-greenhouses (Accessed: January 15th, 2021).

CENTRO COMERCIAL
EL EJIDO
YARA
Knowledge grows
Cuida de lo que más te importa
YaraVita™
STARPHOS
El Fósforo más eficaz en condiciones adversas.

How can this system be seen as economically and environmentally promising? I think it is important to underline what it really means to be hosting the so-called vegetable garden of Europe in Almería and its region. Almería receives 3,000 hours of sunshine per year. But the sun is not enough to grow plants: water is also fundamental. Almería, however, is one of the driest areas, not only of the Iberian Peninsula but of entire Europe, with some of the lowest levels of rainfall. Water resources are very scarce here. So, how did this European vegetable garden come into being in this precise location despite the lack of water? By overexploiting groundwater in aquifers. That is a fact: Almería depends on the plundering of water, a precious resource for future generations. At present, there are areas in the region where water extraction is three times greater than water inflow: water reserves do not have time to regenerate. And because these aquifers are located in coastal areas, the seawater enters the reserves leading to the salinisation of freshwater. Producers claim that drip systems allow for rigorous water control, and this is partly true, but water resources in the region are so limited that it is not enough to satisfy the disproportionate needs of the agro-industry. To give you a concrete example, 500 km away from Almería, in the region of Huelva – one of Europe's leading regions for the cultivation of berries – thousands of hectares of strawberries and red fruits are cultivated industrially. The area literally circles the Doñana National Park [a UNESCO World Heritage Site and sanctuary for migratory birds]. In addition to all this, there are many illegal wells and several hectares of land cultivated without permits – that represent the size of approximately 1,500 football fields – including areas of precious forest floor. The water used for all these crops comes from the aquifer on which the fauna and flora of the park rely. At present, this fauna and flora, which is unique in Europe, is dangerously threatened. From an environmental perspective, another dark side of the Mar de plástico 'model' is the waste it produces. Each year, billions of plastic particles – coming in particular from greenhouse tarpaulins, cans of phytosanitary products, sachets of fertilisers – are found in spring water and in the Mediterranean Sea. There are also huge quantities of pesticide residues contained in uprooted plants left to rot on the ground at the end of each production cycle that seep into the ground and into the groundwater.[124]

TL Some of the vegetables produced in the Almería region are labelled and exported as 'organic'. But can we really still talk of organic products when knowing of the extreme exploitation/pollution of the land?

JMM That's right: at the moment Spain is Europe's leading producer of organic fruits and vegetables, and much of that comes from the region of Almería. This agro-industrial model, whether it be conventional or organic, is based on an intensive system of monocultures. The varieties produced – most of which are not from the region – were created by multinational seed companies and are completely standardised. How can such products be carrying labels that advocate respect for Nature? On top of this, it is operating an economic system entirely based on exports: 80% of the region's agro-industrialists export their products to European countries such as Germany, France, Belgium, Switzerland, Italy, Poland and the United Kingdom. How can a tomato, which must travel 2,000 kilometres or so before arriving on a supermarket shelf, be labelled as organic? All these inconsistencies must be pointed out.

TL What about the agricultural workers that make this system possible?

JMM 80%, not to say 90% of the people who work in the greenhouses are of foreign origin. The migrant workforce in Almería consists of around 100,000 people who mostly come from Morocco,

124 "Officially, the increasing amounts of pesticides and chemical fertilizers, contaminated vegetable waste – over 700,000 tonnes per year – and garbage plastic are collected for "recycling," which tends to include various combinations of composting, burning, and shredding." Christ (2013).

and sub-Saharan countries such as Mali, Guinea and Senegal. Many have reached the Spanish coast with *pateras* [small makeshift boats] and many have died trying to do so. Others come from Poland, and Romania, but also from Latin America. Among them are many women. They have left their country to escape either conflicts or poverty. Generally, these men and women arrive with serious handicaps, in particular, due to a high illiteracy rate and their inability to speak the local language, Castilian. I say handicap because this language deficiency runs counter to their social inclusion. It also accentuates the phenomenon of exploitation at work: imagine not understanding what you are told, not understanding what is written on your employment contract and having to sign it nevertheless...

TL And the Spaniards in all this?

JMM I have been in Almería for three and a half years, and I must admit that I see very few Spaniards in the greenhouses. The local Spanish population looking for a job enter this sector only as a last resort and generally prefer to avoid it because they know that it is one of the worst paid sectors and that it means hours and hours of work.

TL What about recruitment methods? I read in a news report that there are roundabouts on which people looking for work wait while employers in their cars circle around to select them. Is this a myth or the reality?

JMM No, this is not a myth. It happens at around 5 a.m. when it is still dark outside. Migrants looking for work line up on these large roundabouts while greenhouse managers in their vans drive around looking for workers. It goes like this: "I need that many people for that amount of days. I pay that much." The first time that I saw that, it made me think of places where prostitutes await clients... There are roundabouts like this everywhere in the area: an example is Campohermoso, in the locality of Níjar, the heart of the organic production in the region. Imagine these people – many of whom are without proper documents – working without a contract, sometimes up to 16 hours a day, from Monday to Sunday, at 5 euros per hour. Many are the victims of xenophobic remarks – Níjar is the bastion of the far-right Spanish party Vox, by the way. And as if that wasn't enough, at the end of the day, these people only have makeshift shelters to sleep in because they were refused an apartment in the city centre, or because of the lack of accommodation centres. Modern slavery, that's what's behind what some call an economic miracle...

TL This is something you were telling me before I started recording our conversation: about the conditions of the dwellings in which all these migrant workers live. I imagine the shelters are built using any material to hand, and I suppose that they are regularly dismantled by the police, right?

JMM There are about 3,000 people living in slums in the region. These slums are made up of small huts built with wooden pallets and plastic waste from the greenhouses. The majority of these slums are inhabited by men, although there are also a few women with young children. There are those who live there because they have no or very little financial means (because they have just arrived); those who work but have not been able to find a flat to rent; and those in a situation of transition, saving the little money they earn to send it to their families. All of these people are extremely vulnerable. When COVID-19 hit, for instance, slum residents were no longer allowed to go outside and, since they are daily workers, they stopped receiving money and no longer had access to basic goods. The situation lasted several weeks... The people living in the slums are also regular victims of fires – whether intentional or accidental – but also of prostitution and alcoholism. Concerning evictions by the police, I remember that in Huelva, a group of ethical consumers had done a crowdfunding to allow the purchase of solar panels to provide the slums with some basic electricity (there is no electricity or running water supply in the slums). Four or five months after the installation of the solar panels, the police came and destroyed everything...

TL At the beginning of our conversation, you mentioned that one of the problems in the Mar de plástico is the use of pesticides. I was wondering whether workers are provided with proper outfits to protect them against the harmful products that they might have to handle?

JMM One of the priorities of the Sat Alméria union is to provide migrant workers with information (labour rights, trade union rights) and language courses. Indeed, most of them do not understand Castilian, and cannot, for example, know the nature of the substances they are asked to spray on the crops. It is very rare that farm managers – conventional or organic ones, as certain pesticides such as copper are authorised in organic farming too – give such information to their employees. The workers are therefore neither informed nor protected. There are regular cases of eye irritation and itchy skin due to direct contact with harmful products. Unfortunately, there is very little research carried out to attest to the links between certain serious diseases and the spreading of pesticides. It is interesting to note that the majority of migrant workers I have met in greenhouses that are certified as 'Organic' or 'Ethical' have absolutely no awareness of what 'organic' or 'conventional' is supposed to mean in terms of working conditions. What they know, however, is that there is no difference for them between working in the organic or the conventional system: the conditions of salary and treatment are the same...

TL Despite the many reports, it seems that few European consumers are aware of the situation.

JMM Yes, and this plunder of Nature and this problem of humans' exploitation are not new. It has been going on for thirty years. This said, there is a relative awareness thanks to the many reports produced by international journalists broadcast on television or radio during peak hours. Of course, the managers of large distribution chains cannot sit idly by and do nothing in the face of such denunciations. Following the broadcast of a report produced by Belgian national radio RTBF, for instance, Carrefour Belgium promised that it would intensify its checks with its Spanish suppliers concerning, in particular, the situation of workers (in terms of compliance with health and safety regulations, etc.). Other big chains such as Aldi, Lidl but also Tesco and Sainsbury's also reacted. There is therefore an awareness that is growing, but mainly abroad.

TL Are these problems relayed by the local and national press nonetheless?

JMM This agricultural model has allowed the development of the local economy. It should not be forgotten that not too long ago, Andalusia was one of the poorest and most disadvantaged regions of Spain, with a very high rate of illiteracy among the local population. Previous Spanish governments, and especially the Spanish right, were therefore reluctant to touch a system that had allowed the whole region to develop. There are very few actions taken to change this so-called model from within. There is also a lot of pressure from lobbying by seed multinationals and phytosanitary companies, and many of those – such as BASF, BAYER/Monsanto, Rijk Zwaan and Syngenta – have their headquarters in Almería. Thus, the local press does not talk about it –

2013

except in extreme cases of suspicious death (asphyxia, heart attack, etc.). Especially because, with the advent of the internet, the press sector increasingly needs financial means to stay alive and local newspapers are financed by the agricultural sector itself through advertisements from producers, fertiliser and pesticide manufacturers, and plastic manufacturers. The press, therefore, avoids pointing the finger at the bad practices of this industry which keeps them alive. Over the past two years, some national newspapers like *El País* started publishing articles on the living conditions of migrant workers in Almería, following the publication of numerous reports made by the international press. At the beginning of 2020, the United Nations Special Rapporteur on Extreme Poverty and Human Rights, Philip Alston came to see the working conditions of agricultural workers in Huelva.[125] In a press conference following the visit, he said the workers are treated worse than animals. This had such an impact that the government of Pedro Sánchez had to react. A few months later, in May 2020, the Spanish Ministry of Labour sent special brigades – made up of the Guardia Civil and the Work Inspection – to assess the situation. There was therefore a certain awareness on the part of the government following the visit of Philip Alston.

TL Have these inspections led to sanctions or the creation of new laws– at the national or European level – to protect agricultural workers and soils?

125 In the report following his visit to Alméria, Philip Alston affirms that: "I also visited areas I suspect many Spaniards would not recognize as a part of their country. A shantytown with far worse conditions than a refugee camp, without running water, electricity, or sanitation, where migrant workers have lived for years without any improvement in their situation. [...] I was struck by the resilience and compassion of the people with whom I met, who showed real generosity by sharing often quite personal experiences with me in order to inform this report". ◊ www.ohchr.org/en/NewsEvents/Pages/DisplayNews.aspx?NewsID=25524&LangID=E (Accessed: January 15th, 2021).

JMM Following the dispatch of the Special Labour Inspection Brigades, the Minister of Labour, Yolanda Diaz, announced that a report would be issued by her ministry announcing the actions it was going to pursue. We are awaiting the report and ministry decisions. What we can announce is that one in three farms inspected (approximately 9,000 inspection visits in 2021) is in a situation of fraud or illegality with respect to labour law but also with respect to human rights.

TL The exploitation of humans and the environment on which this 'model' is based guarantees ever lower prices for the vegetables and fruits found on supermarket shelves. Do you think that Spanish and more broadly European consumers have a role to play in encouraging change?

JMM We are faced with a production system that is only viable thanks to this 'low-cost' labour. The producers admit it themselves: if they paid according to what the law says, they would have to close down their businesses, because the prices offered by the purchasing centres are always lower while the costs of production (inputs, seeds, plastics, etc.) are constantly increasing. To conclude, I would say that before being consumers we are people, human beings: the problem is not whether as consumers we can change things, the problem is whether as people we want to change things.

Bright Nights. Greenhouses and Light Pollution

d-o-t-s in conversation with Charlène Flores and Ken Walczak[126]
photos by Charlène Flores

According to the International Dark-Sky Association, "light pollution is increasing worldwide at twice the rate of global population growth." For that reason it has become an issue in cities, but also in rural areas where large industrial greenhouses are lighten up day and night. French photographer Charlène Flores, author of the photo-reportage titled *The Northern Lights of Agriculture* (2019) and Ken Walczak, Senior Manager of research program Far Horizons at the Adler Planetarium in Chicago converse on the consequences of this little known phenomenon and call for a new appreciation of darkness.

d-o-t-s To start the conversation, Ken, could you tell us how/why you first decided to focus on the topic of light pollution in your research?

Ken Walczak I work at the Adler Planetarium in Chicago, collaborating with students, astronomers and researchers on hands-on science and engineering experiments. We have been launching high-altitude balloons to the Stratosphere for about fourteen years now. You get an amazing view as you are fundamentally at the edge of space. Flights usually take place during the day. One thing that we never did was to fly at night. So about five or six years ago we decided to do a nighttime flight. We were wondering what to look for at night, and we realised we could simply look 'down' at the Earth. I have always been passionate

126 Zoom conversation recorded by d-o-t-s on November 23rd, 2021.

about astronomy and obviously the Planetarium as an institution is all about connecting people to the universe, so if we can't observe the universe it is hard to raise the argument that we should be concerned or interested about our place in it. Light pollution, we thought, was a perfect line of inquiry for us. That's how we started designing a system that maps light pollution from the Stratosphere. Once we started doing that it got us even more connected with that issue and the light pollution research community because what we were doing was unique.

d-o-t-s On our side, we approached light pollution in the frame of our investigation about commercial greenhouses and their effects on the environment. Something that surprised us was that, despite the fact that it is widely known (and visible) that big greenhouses have an effect on light pollution, it was hard to find relevant scientific data on the matter. Most of the papers that we came across focused, for instance, on the light emitted by big cities. In your articles, however, you argue that industrial greenhouses are a good example of "excessive" sources of disturbance in the rural context. Why specifically should we worry about their light emissions and their effects on rural zones?

KW I stumbled upon the issue of industrial greenhouses because I was looking at sources of light pollution through satellite data and I noticed these sources of light – visible to the naked eye – that were very odd because they were not in the city and were very concentrated but incredibly strong. Because it was so shocking and so surprising, I asked myself how prevalent these greenhouses are. So I started, just by eye, looking through the world map to find these sources of light pollution. I am now working with a data scientist to create a citizen science project to not only qualify and find all the light pollution sources emitted by greenhouses but also other unique sources around the world beyond city limits, to see where the problems are coming from. By far, the light produced by greenhouses is the one that stands out because it is so strong. By nature of the commercial greenhouses industry, these structures – I am not talking about family greenhouses in backyards, but about greenhouse complexes that spread on hectares and hectares – need essentially two things: relatively cheap land and access to power. A lot of power. So they cannot be in a remote location but they cannot be in a town or a city either because the land is too expensive. So, by nature, they tend to be in that divide between the countryside and the urban environments. In general, we always think of light pollution as an urban issue, but in reality, the more sensitive locations for ecological or even health effects are rural areas. At the Adler Planetarium, we are working with some urban ecologists who are helping qualify and monitor which species actually thrive in an urban environment, and it is definitely not as diverse as in what we consider as a relatively untainted environment. Light does have a huge effect on insect populations, bird populations and especially migrating birds, and on just about every element of the living ecological system. So when you introduce to a relatively un-light-polluted environment a source that is so bright, it is like using an arc lamp as a reading light. It is excessive. And that is what happens in some of these rural environments.

d-o-t-s What about you, Charlène, how did you come across the subject of greenhouses in your work?

Charlène Flores A friend of mine, who works as a farmer next to my home town in Brittany (France), told me about this strange pink sky at night. I didn't really believe her until, one day, she sent me a picture of it at midnight. I was based in Paris at the time, and I thought that the situation was so weird that I needed to take a look at it. So I decided to take a train to go and see it with my own eyes. When I arrived there – it was at the end of December, I recall – the place was neon pink! The whole village where the greenhouses are located was completely covered with this light. It was so strange. There was no information or explanation whatsoever to be found anywhere about the origin of this light. I searched on the internet, on social networks. Nothing. So I decided to investigate and soon discovered that this light was coming from a greenhouse producing tomatoes. I also found out that, at the time, 80% of the tomato production in France came from Brittany, one of the rainiest regions in the country – not the region you would spontaneously associate with tomato production. The tomatoes are grown in industrial greenhouses and I started to talk with some astrophysicists and other people about the light that was emitted by them.

KW Charlène, have you talked to researchers within the Dark-Sky community?

CF Yes, I spoke with Sébastien Vauclair, a French astrophysicist who studies light pollution. He helped me a lot to understand the impact of light pollution on the environment and on all living beings. We have the tendency to solely talk about insects and migratory birds, but humans too are impacted, and so are plants. Everyone, basically. In fact, something I learnt while researching this topic is that tomatoes need the artificial light to be turned off regularly, for at least 24 hours, otherwise it is too demanding and exhausting for them to grow constantly. Even plants need to rest!

d-o-t-s For the record, before we started recording the conversation, Charlène, you said that the complex of greenhouses that you investigated in your photo documentary emits 60 times more light than Rennes, the nearest city, which has 217,728 inhabitants. How did the inhabitants of La Chapelle-des-Fougeretz (the town where the site is located) feel about this situation? Were the greenhouses perceived as a plus – as a source of jobs, for instance – or rather as a nuisance – as a source of diseases – for example?

CF It wasn't easy to meet people, because you are there at night and obviously people are asleep. But people who live very near to the greenhouses in La Chapelle-des-Fougeretz told me that the worst isn't actually the light, but the noise. Because at night, when the whole complex is lit up, cocks are crowing as if it was dawn all night. When taking pictures, I would always have my recorder on: it really felt like daytime. Regarding the issue of diseases, it is hard to actually trace back and link the source of an illness to the light pollution. In France, LED lights – the type of lights that are used in commercial greenhouses – haven't been around for long enough yet. People working in the industry tend to say that LED light is great because it is cheap and it consumes less energy. This is true, but as it is more powerful than a regular light, its impact is probably greater.

d-o-t-s What about the owner(s) of the greenhouses, did you manage to talk to them during your investigation?

CF It was complicated meeting people who were working in or who owned the greenhouses. The owners were very reluctant to talk because they felt that anyway I was going to portray them as 'the bad ones', and obviously they were not completely wrong. So, many declined my request to talk. One, however, did agree to meet me and showed me the inside of a greenhouse. It was very interesting to discover that it is not just about light. Light, in fact, isn't enough for tomatoes to grow fast. It is also about heating the place and feeding the crops. As for the people working in the greenhouses, a lot of them are migrant workers, so they don't really want to talk, because they are simply scared and some are working there illegally.

KW I haven't visited one of these locations yet: I have always seen them from above! I am curious to know how it feels when you are there? Because it does seem more pervasive than just a pink sky.

CF It's a bit like being in a David Lynch movie. It looks familiar, but it isn't. It is quite surreal. Most of the time there is no one around, but you know, it is a village so there are houses, so sometimes I would see someone coming home late. Technically it was also quite complicated to get the right colour with my camera because I really wanted to show what my eyes were seeing, and at night it can be tricky. I actually had to tell magazines that my pictures had not been photoshopped! The fog – which in Brittany you get almost every night – helped densify the light, you could almost touch it. Strangely, the people who live there seem to get used to it all very quickly. When I showed them the images many of them told me that they actually had not realised how weird this was.

KW I am also a delegate to the International Dark-Sky Association and I work on ways to communicate the impact of light pollution and try to bridge that gap between the data and the real story. One of the things I find interesting is that our eyes are amazing tools. They have about nine orders of magnitude of sensitivity range: from literally less than a lux to bright daylight but any one time our eyes are about four orders of magnitude of range. So that's why if you go outside on a nice dark night even one street light can shift your perception. Even one light can become a shifting window. Eyes are so adaptive. This is why I was wondering about the visual feeling of the experience. But I am surprised to hear that the people who live there have been able to adapt so quickly, merely because night by night you don't realise how different it is until you see how different it can be...

d-o-t-s Charlène, was the purpose of your investigation also, in some ways, to denounce the situation? Do you know if your reportage has had an effect locally? Did it help the general public to be more aware of the issue?

CF At first, I didn't want to denounce anything because I basically didn't know what was going on. It took me some time to understand where it was coming from, what it really was, and the consequences it had. I didn't know all of that when I started. I just saw this incredible pink sky and that was it. But the more I was discovering, the more I became convinced that this reportage could have repercussions. And it did. When the photos were published in the weekly French news magazine *L'Obs,* a lot of TV people called me and went to this particular village to report as well. I went back to La Chapelle-des-Fougeretz one year later to talk to people I had met before, and to see the greenhouses. In the meantime, the Green Party had won the local elections and had pressured the owner of the greenhouses to install black panels to cover the light emitted by the greenhouses.

d-o-t-s Ken, what would you say is the best way to raise awareness of the danger of something that people get used to so easily or simply can't totally grasp?

KW A lot of our students come from the city of Chicago and many of them have never experienced a natural night sky. So one of the things that we do at the beginning of our programme is to load all the kids up in a bus, we drive the closest we can to a relatively dark sky site and the experience is amazing. One time we went to a National Park not far from the Planetarium, and some students were afraid to get out of the bus literally because there was no light. They always equate darkness with danger and light with safety. (By the way, we perceive light as safe but if you look at the data, it isn't true.) We had to convince them that it was fine. On some occasions, students even broke down in tears after finally stepping out of the bus because they had never seen a starry sky ever. I bet that if you came to Chicago, you would be shocked because it is much brighter than any European city. But we are used to it here, that's the problem.

d-o-t-s What are the goals of the Dark-Sky movement? And what tools are put in place to achieve that?

KW As I said, we do a lot of education and outreach. The idea is not simply to turn out lights, it is about using them sensibly, and communicating that more isn't always better. Charlène was talking earlier about the colours of the lights. Perhaps you know that the blue light frequencies are the most impactful, especially biologically for humans. A little more than a decade ago researchers discovered that we actually have a third kind of receptor in our eyes that regulates our circadian rhythm and it is very sensitive to blue because blue is naturally an indicator of daylight. So when our body perceives blue light through this unique perceptor, it basically tells our body that it is daylight...

CF Yes, and this is the problem with industrial greenhouses right now because they use LED light with blue light for the crops. Some scientists have discovered that depending on the light you use the growth of the plants will be different. For instance, if you use a green light the plant will be smaller, but if you mix red and blue the crops – at least tomatoes – grow faster and bigger. Like so, they can harvest tomatoes every seven weeks, even in Brittany, during the cold season.

d-o-t-s Greenhouses like the ones in La Chapelle-des-Fougeretz are booming. In an article on darkskies.org, Ken, you write that the 2020 Global Commercial Greenhouse Industry Report projected "the global market for Commercial Greenhouse[s] estimated at US$26.4 Billion in the year 2020, is projected to reach... US$43.8 Billion by 2027, growing at a [compound annual growth rate] of 7.5%." Why should we be alarmed by these numbers?[127] What does this boom mean for human and non-human beings?

KW As Charlène was saying, the efficiency of LEDs is why industrial greenhouses are now affordable and efficient enough that they have become so large. A century ago, you could control the environment, but the sunlight was what you wanted. No one ever thought of using a greenhouse to grow in a dark or cloudy environment! So, it was the LED light technology that made this 24 hours and 365 days a year cycle possible. But, we cannot simply move forward because we have an efficient tool without thinking of the consequences first. And this is what I am worried about with the use of LED lights. I think we need a balanced approach. There are technologies – such as the black curtains that Charlène mentioned – that can be used at night. It's true that they are relatively expensive, but on the other side who's going to pay the price of not installing them: the health of the local communities, the environment? Greenhouses are amazing and enable us to produce vegetables in locations where it would have never been possible before, but maybe these places are not the best places to grow tomatoes. Maybe there are other crops to grow there that are less energy-intensive. Greenhouses are great because they provide a fully controlled environment. In some of the greenhouses that I know, here in the US, they wouldn't even let you go in, unless you wear something like a biological suit, because they don't want any pests or disease. And that in a sense is great because you don't have to worry about losing crops because of fungus or potential disease, plus you don't have to use pesticides. But the trade-off is immense. Greenhouses require a lot of energy: the amount of carbon emission you need to match the energy provided by the sun

127 According to biology PhD researcher Douglas Boyes from the university of Newcastle, "Between 2012 and 2016, satellite measurements revealed that the global area polluted by artificial light grew by 2% each year, intruding ever deeper into biodiversity hotspots like tropical forests", in Boyes, D. "Why the changing colour of our streetlights could be a danger for insect populations", in *The Conversation*, August 21st, 2021. ◊ theconversation.com/why-the-changing-colour-of-our-streetlights-could-be-a-danger-for-insect-populations-166470 (Accessed: October 18th, 2021).

(about 1300 watts per square metre) is immense. True LEDs are made more efficient so it is now more cost-effective. But we have to think about the downstream impacts.

CF While producing my photo reportage, I asked one owner of greenhouses in Brittany why he started growing crops like that. And he told me: "Well, because people are asking for cherry tomatoes for Christmas." If we could just try to consume differently, greenhouses such as the one in La Chapelle-des-Fougeretz would no longer be necessary. Also, what's interesting is that usually after about two years, 20% of the LED lights in a greenhouse need to be replaced. It's a lot. In Europe, 98% of the lights that are used are produced in China. So if there would be an issue with the supply chain one day, what would become of the greenhouses and of the tomatoes?

KW I think that what you documented, Charlène, is an example of sort of getting the point across that it is not being done right at this point.

d-o-t-s Yes, and that takes us to the last point we would like to discuss with you: the importance of creatives in the visualisation and translation of scientific data or facts.

KW We do capture dramatic observations over night skies. We developed an all-sky camera that you put out at night and pick it up in the morning and it creates images of the sky through the night. And it is one of those examples of when we show a visual of the night-time sky of Chicago, like a timelapse. It is pretty dramatic. You see clouds moving over and the change of light throughout the night. This allows us to show what the night looks like from a different perspective and it definitely opens eyes. One of the things we've done is take the same camera to a pristine night sky and if you do a side by side, you realise that the time-lapse of Chicago's sky at night looks like daytime. You can't experience

within one night a beautiful milky way coming on from the horizon in a city so easily, so how else are you going to communicate that? You need visuals, you need ways to connect with the environment. And I think what you did, Charlène, with your pictures and what we are trying to do with visual data and our observation of the Stratosphere is to present them in ways that are visually stunning and I think that this attracts attention and helps people be aware.

CF Light pollution was not even a topic for the French Ministry of Ecology, Sustainable Development and Energy until very recently. But there is a growing awareness of the topic right now. And I think that is the key: spreading the word about the consequences of light pollution, and how we can play our part as well, as citizens. After seeing my photos, a lot of people told me that they had stopped eating tomatoes in the winter. Many of them admitted that they were not aware of the fact that tomatoes couldn't actually grow during winter, or at least they had forgotten about it. I think people are so disconnected from natural cycles nowadays, but the more we talk about this, the more people will think about it. A still image can be so much more powerful than seeing the thing with your own eyes.

KW Yes, once you have become aware of it, you simply can't unsee it. Light is essential for life. But why do we assume darkness isn't? This natural cycle has been going on forever, and in less than a century we have changed it completely and we don't even know what the implications are yet.

IV. Stories of Renewal

Normally dedicated to plant cultivation, in some cases greenhouses also become fertile spaces for the empowerment of human communities. Testifying to acts of reclamation, reconnection, diversification, and remembrance, the texts that follow show how radical and contextualised practices can help restore broken relationships with the land and its inhabitants, be they humans or other-than-humans.

Nurturing Community

an essay by d-o-t-s

In 2021, the St Andrews Botanic Garden in Scotland launched *The Tangled Bank*, a project aimed at reshaping parts of its garden. The goal was the recreation of local biotopes currently under threat – like sand dunes and meadows – and the repurposing of existing buildings to construct Climate Change-resilient habitats, capable of reducing the Botanic Garden's carbon footprint as well as its use of water and pest control. As part of this project, it was decided to fully remove nine of the ten greenhouses present onsite and to repurpose the last one – which has a footprint of over 400 m^2 – converting it into a pergola. The plan was to remove the glass panels and the glazing bars, thus allowing native climbing plants to grow over the bare structure, and the new area was called *The Climbing Garden*.

"It was a challenge to convince people that it was a good idea!" explains the Director of the St Andrews Botanic Garden, landscape architect Harry Watkins. "Lots of botanic gardens have historic iron or timber-framed glasshouses which have a very stylised design language, but ours was from the 1970s and was very much a 'working' glasshouse, so it's a bit different to what people might imagine,"[128] adds Watkins. "Now that we have taken the glass off the frame and identified which plants can survive the winter without protection," he continues, "we can begin the process of preparing the wire frame and selecting plants. From an experiential perspective, this opens unusual and exciting opportunities.

128 Personal conversation, May 11th, 2022.

With no glass on the frame, people will be able to walk 'through the walls' of the pergola and into other parts of the garden in ways that weren't possible previously, and open up new sight lines or frame views of specific trees. Our hope is that the climbing plants create a shaded and more humid environment within the pergola, so people visiting it will feel like they are in this green cocoon which changes the ways they see the rest of the garden."[129]

As the energy consumption of glasshouses in botanical gardens is questioned by some,[130] the bold shift of paradigm proposed by the St Andrews Botanic Garden suggests novel educational scenarios that could be adopted by other botanical institutions too. By 'undressing' them, in fact, scientific greenhouses can move from being bubbles where visitors witness the 'exotic' to spaces where the public is invited to *re*discover[131] the specificities of the local flora and actively question our responsibilities as a species.

Converting greenhouses into something different by fully embracing their educational potential is what many art collectives and citizen initiatives have also been doing all around the world. From Casablanca to Brussels, from London to San Francisco, artists, associations, curators, and cooks have reclaimed glasshouses and polytunnels

129 Personal conversation, May 11th, 2022.

130 A recent example is the tropical greenhouse of the Botanic Garden of the Jardin des Plantes, in Lille (France), which was closed down in September 2022 by the municipality because "The building alone accounts for 1.14% of the city's energy consumption. So the municipality decided to close it. [...] It is one of the most energy-intensive buildings in our city.", in A. Delcourt, L. Beunaiche, A. Morvan, R. Maucort, "Énergie : la serre équatoriale du Jardin des plantes de Lille ferme", *France Info*, September 21st, 2022. ◊ www.francetvinfo.fr/meteo/climat/energie-la-serre-equatoriale-du-jardin-des-plantes-de-lille-ferme_5372971.html (Accessed: June 18th, 2023).

131 French philosopher Bruno Latour claims that "Belonging to a territory does not at all mean a return to the land, it is a discovery, an invention. There is therefore an enormous work of reappropriation to be done, by the sciences, of what is, for example, a soil, a watershed, a biotope. It is the discovery of a new world, hence the analogy I draw with the century of great discoveries", in "Bruno Latour: 'Avec le réchauffement, le sol se dérobe sous nos pieds à tous'", *Libération*, March 16th, 2018. ◊ www.liberation.fr/debats/2018/03/16/bruno-latour-avec-le-rechauffement-le-sol-se-derobe-sous-nos-pieds-a-tous_1636709/ (Accessed: January 15th, 2022).

transforming them into fertile environments for cultivating and propagating new ideas. The transparent and accessible character of these structures provide the ideal canvasses for debates and negotiations to happen, fostering inclusion and diversity, and providing communities with spaces where the future can be collectively imagined and built.

La Serre (Casablanca, Morocco)

In that sense, the initiative led by the artist Mohamed Fariji with the cultural association L'Atelier de l'Observatoire in Casablanca, Morocco, constitutes an interesting case study. Entitled *La Serre* (meaning *greenhouse*, in French), the project consists of a mobile and light polytunnel – covering an area of up to 200 m^2 – that since 2015 has been deployed in diverse public urban spaces and rural areas. Once installed, "it is simply there, and quickly takes its place in the panorama of a street, a park or even a rooftop,"[132] affirms Sabrina Kamili, the Moroccan-Italian cultural entrepreneur who worked for L'Atelier de l'Observatoire and was in charge of budget preparation, fundraising, logistics and programming for the installation of the structure. Beside being flexible and relatively cheap to set up, according to Kamili the structure, thanks to its permeable and accessible appearance, is a powerful ephemeral mediation device. "Because, in the end," Kamili continues, "it is always easier to take the plunge and enter a polytunnel than crossing the large intimidating white walls of a building with inscriptions that say, in French,[133] 'cultural centre'." Once inside the semi-circular structure, visitors are greeted without fuss, as "it is cosy, yet not luxurious nor perfectly well set up." A small library, an area to drink tea and a space to host conferences

132 Personal conversation, April 2022.

133 Described as the language "of the other," French was introduced in Morocco during the French Protectorate (1912-1956). Reminiscent of the colonial past, it is perceived as "elitist" and has enjoyed "for a long time [...] a privileged status, being associated with knowledge and openness to others, to Europe.", in Ziamari, K., Jaap De Ruiter, J., "Les langues au Maroc : réalités, changements et évolutions linguistiques", Dupret, B., Rhani, Z., Boutaleb, A., Ferrié, J-N., ed., *Le Maroc au présent: D'une époque à l'autre, une société en mutation.* New edition [online]. Casablanca: Centre Jacques-Berque, (2015, generated March 18th, 2022). ◊ www.doi.org/10.4000/books.cjb.990 (Accessed: March 18th, 2022).

and roundtables set the tone of the participatory events – conferences, roundtables, exhibitions, and screenings – that the cultural association L'Atelier de l'Observatoire organises inside it. Moving away from the institutional and dominant visions that characterise the local cultural scene, *La Serre* welcomes everyone, from local inhabitants and students, to artists and researchers. Offering favourable conditions for the blossoming of original artistic and cultural ventures, the polytunnel promotes the birth of new projects and new voices and invites everyone to engage collectively.

Parckfarm (Brussels, Belgium)

Embracing the strength of the collective is also one of the aims of Parckfarm, in Brussels, Belgium. Managed by the eponymous association, the project's headquarter is a multi-function horticultural glasshouse with two slender naves and compact volume, located in the Park L28, an ancient freight station now transformed into a green space, in the Molenbeek-Saint-Jean district. Designed by Belgian architect Bert Gellynck, the greenhouse was installed in 2014, on the occasion of the 2014 Parckdesign Festival, an event focusing on food production and urban farming. "The space of the greenhouse was chosen to be the heart of the festival, a place for meetings, exchanges, and the reception of the public with a small cafeteria and catering," explains Stéphanie Bertel, who works for the association being in charge of its coordination, volunteering and communication. "During the 5 months of the festival, we also organised a lot of know-how exchange workshops there, calling for the participation of the local population. The enthusiasm of the inhabitants and their involvement were such that they formed an association with the intention of perpetuating the project." Since then, the greenhouse has become a precious meeting point for the local community. " We want to become a real place of education, creation of citizen projects in tune with our values of resilience, respect for the environment and also a place where we create links and solidarity to consider our world in all its complexity,"[134] Bertel adds.

134 Personal conversation, April 2022.

The success of the project might have to do with the structure's transparency and apparent lightness. Passing by, one can see the volunteers inside, busy behind the DIY counter preparing beverages and dishes, or animating hands-on initiation workshops on herbalism, cooking, gardening and more. Meanwhile visitors sip elderberry syrup on the terrace, and local residents harvest mugwort in the small community garden and in the orchard planted next to the greenhouse. Everything seems connected and fluid: one can see through the permeable architecture as much as pass through it. Yet, the greenhouse is not a corridor but rather operates as a parenthesis with a metamorphosing effect: after having learnt something or met someone new, one comes out of it enriched and transformed. "Indeed, Bertel confirms, these community spaces allow meeting and exchange. Doing it together strengthens the bonds. The combined actions of gardening with a place for environmental education such as Parckfarm is intended to reinforce ecological values, respect for the environment and also for humans a nd other living beings. That being said, it's a long-term job. This weaving of links is subtle, fragile, always to be reinvented and accompanied." But this transparency, so favourable for plants' cultivation, comes with downsides. Suggesting that glasshouses might not be the most judicious choice when it comes to creating a permanent gathering place, Stéphanie Bertel points out several issues. The interior overheats when it is sunny outside, and "the greenhouse must be shaded with lime (it helps...); it is cold in the winter, and impossible to heat; it is rudimentary in terms of cosiness; it is easily subject to intrusions, especially in the context of a public park that does not close at night; and it is also fragile."

Rochester Square (London, UK)

A metallic chassis frames the wild-looking garden of nasturtiums, pink yarrows and multicolor larkspurs that welcomes the visitors at Rochester Square Garden, a cultural and community-based project, in the heart of one of London's most vibrant districts, Camden Town. The sole remains of an old plant nursery that closed down in the 1980s, the chassis of the former greenhouses is “the most iconic image of Rochester Square, it’s featured in most of our photos!”[135] affirms Francesca Anfossi who, together with her partner Eric Wragge, started the project back in 2016. Merging gardening, ceramics and food, the venture has been slowly developing since, and is being positively received by both local residents and the art community. “Throughout the last five years, many local residents have been visiting, eating, cooking and gardening here. There is a constant coming and going of people and a very supportive group of artists suggesting projects and developing small and big ideas – both inside the warehouse and outside in the garden areas,” explains Anfossi. “My main vision for Rochester Square,” adds the Italian artist, “came from a trip I made to India some years ago. I was fascinated by the system there of recycling clay teacups: they are fired at very low temperatures, making them so friable that they can easily be turned back into soil when smashed to the ground after use. The soil is then used again to make new teacups. This image really stuck with me and guides me in my approach to Rochester Square: a sort of creative earth cycle from soil (clay) to plants (food) to plates (eating).”

Offering a wide range of facilities – such as a bright fully equipped ceramic workshop, and a community garden – and activities like ceramic workshops for adults and kids, garden courses, art residencies, collaborations with companies and art schools, etc., Rochester Square also hosts regular communal dinners served in ceramic tableware. “It was important for us to try different things around these three elements (clay, food, garden),” highlights Anfossi, “in order to figure out what works and also to create a community. Rochester Square is quite unique in that way, we don’t just facilitate, we connect people, and lots of connections are made over our large seasonal dinners and informal lunches.” Thanks to all this, the place has been “very successful in bringing people from the local community, to slow down, get to know each other and share thoughts and ideas together.”

135 Personal conversation, May 2023.

The Greenhouse Project (San Francisco, USA)

Back in the 1920s, the multicultural Portola neighbourhood, in San Francisco, was home to a flourishing flower-growing business run by the Garibaldi family. For over seven decades, a complex of wooden greenhouses was used by the Garibaldis to grow roses and snapdragons, as well as "dahlias, delphinium, French marigolds, pansies, coreopsis and several other varieties."[136] Abandoned in the 1990s, the site has since become an attractive spot for developers seeking vacant lots in the increasingly expensive San Francisco area. But a large development project would deprive the local community of a rare open land. An inconceivable scenario for the inhabitants who have been campaigning for years to save the memory of this historic site and turn it back into a long-lasting living place. Arguing that the current "food system is broken," the local organisation The Greenhouse Project – which is working in tandem with other NGOs such as Friends of 770 Woolsey – hopes to reduce the distance between farms and people by turning the site into an urban farm, where the community could grow its own food. With the risk of green gentrification in mind, Elisa Laird, a member of Friends of 770 Woolsey explains: "Neighbourhood residents and leaders have been consistently outspoken and proactive about their interest in developing a community asset at the site since at least 2013. [...] A robust community outreach process is vital, to help mitigate the potential impacts of gentrification on this majority lower income neighbourhood. For years we have held weekend community events, such as Earth Day celebrations, that bring neighbours together."[137] The ancient greenhouses are at the heart of this process. Appearing in the opening scene of *The Last Black Man in San Francisco* (Joe Talbot, 2019) – a film that deals precisely with the issue of gentrification – they have become "a community totem for what gentrification should

136 "University Mound Nursery/770 Woolsey Street", San Francisco Landmark Designation Report, February 21st, 2019. ◊ static1.squarespace.com/static/608d51e7568bce1648f37d01/t/60a9a1fdf-1f34945c7e4f88f/1621729809264/770%2BWoolsey%2BLandmark%2BDesignation%2BReport.pdf (Accessed: February 12th, 2022).

137 Personal conversation, May 2022.

and shouldn't be,"[138] states writer Meka Boyle in an article written in March 2022 in which she gives an account of the endeavour of local organisations to save the place from being torn down. Contrary to the current trend valuing temporary occupations, for the local inhabitants to get involved on the long run, argue the members of The Greenhouse Project and Friends of 770 Woolsey, the access to the land needs to be secured. Thus a fundraising campaign was launched. "If we raise enough funds to acquire the entire property, we will restore/rebuild/replace all structures, plus add more. The community will be consulted and their priorities will be taken into primary consideration," explained Laird. "If we raise just part of the funds, the agreement with the developers allows us to buy 40% of the land. If we fail to raise sufficient funds to purchase any land, the developers have agreed to restore 2 greenhouses plus the 'boiler house' on a corner (consisting of 17% of the total property) to U.S. Department of the Interior standards for historic preservation. So, the 'worst case' is that we have saved a small corner of the historic property, and the 'best case' is that we can restore all 2.2 acres of it,"[139] Elisa Laird affirmed, hopeful.

Le Serre dei Giardini (Bologna, Italy)

Exploring other funding methods – merging private and public resources – the project Le Serre dei Giardini (meaning *the greenhouses of the gardens*, in Italian) is a hybrid venture investing in artistic production and research, well-being and diversification as ways to respond to the challenges presented by unemployment, the decline in public welfare, and the current redefinition of work (e.g. telecommuting) in Italy. The large complex where Le Serre dei Giardini is set was originally built in the early 20th century as part of the Giardini Margherita, a public park in the city of Bologna, Italy. It featured several glasshouses, diverse horticultural infrastructures and offices for the park's gardeners. Left in a completely

138 ◊ www.kneedeeptimes.org/portola-garden-district-returns-to-its-roots/ (Accessed: February 12th, 2022).

139 Personal conversation, May 2022.

derelict state by the municipality for many years due to the lack of finances, the site was finally given under concession for 15 years to Kilowatt, a Bolognese working cooperative, which undertook to regenerate it, investing 2 million euros with the support of the Emilia Romagna Region in 2015 and 2021.

Determined to give the site back to the city after years of abandonment, Kilowatt transformed the former complex into a cultural hub. Many of the original features of the old site were preserved and repurposed. The main greenhouse became a bar for the summer; the gardeners' technical rooms – with their bright yellow facades – now host a co-working area and a day nursery that welcomes children from 0 to 6 years old; the concrete seedbeds were transformed into open-air sitting areas; the seedlings' nurseries are now a large vegetable garden that provides fresh herbs for the glasshouse-bistro while offering an open-air classroom for the children of the childcare centre to get to learn about plants. Visitors and co-workers are invited to relax and enjoy the fresh air on the wooden platforms among the growing vegetables and fruits. "The space is open to anyone: both entrance and the cultural events are free of charge. This means that Le Serre dei Giardini is a mutable place that changes its appearance and type of audience between morning and evening,"[140] explains Giulia Quattrini who is part of Kilowatt's team. Le Serre dei Giardini is also an artistic centre that organises art residencies. "In 2021, we won another tender for the allocation of the last abandoned greenhouses to bring a new project new project to life. Called Serra Madre, it is meant to be the home of artists who want to be catalysts for change, critical observers of the present, and key players in imagining and building sustainable futures," concludes Quattrini.

Mediamatic (Amsterdam, The Netherlands)

The dedication to socially urgent themes, multidisciplinary creativity, and open-ended experimentations are the traits that define Mediamatic,

140 Personal conversation, May 2023.

a hybrid cultural hub located in the revivified port area of the Eastern Docklands, in Amsterdam, The Netherlands. Set in an ancient brick warehouse flanked by two long greenhouses overlooking the city's canals, Mediamatic features a plant-based restaurant, an aquaponics farm, a mycelium lab, and hosts a rich programme of events and hands-on workshops. Offering an open platform to emerging designers, makers and chefs eager to test new artistic concepts and formats, over the years Mediamatic – which was founded in 1983 in Groningen, and moved to Amsterdam in 1986 changing location several times – has been addressing topics as diverse as the future of food, multispecies inclusiveness, death and funeral traditions, scent, invasive plants and biomaterials.

According to Italian food designer Giulia Soldati – who worked there between 2018 and 2021 – "Mediamatic is a place that fully embraces experimentation. As a creative, you know that you can approach them with concepts out of the ordinary. The two founders are at the same time crazy and brave: they want Mediamatic to provoke debates and to do so they welcome ideas that others might see as absurd or unachievable."[141] As Soldati points out, "they receive public funding from different sources,[142] and they use that money to push ideas further." The food designer also highlights how Mediamatic's ETEN restaurant – which is hosted in one of the long greenhouses – "constitutes a meaningful experience for both the staff and the guests. You work in an open kitchen, and thus have a constant unfiltered contact with the clients. The transparent architecture also creates a positive feeling of being part of a bigger ecosystem: you are connected to the people, the building itself and the surrounding landscape. When you cook, you have in front of you the water of Amsterdam's

141 Personal conversation, September 2023.
142 Mediamatic is sponsored by Mondriaan Fonds, Stimuleringsfonds voor de Creatieve Industrie and Amsterdams Fonds voor de Kunst ◊ www.mediamatic.net/en/page/10341/about-mediamatic (Accessed: September 11th, 2023).

canals, while to the side you can see the other greenhouse where the aquaponic system is installed and the herbs are cultivated. You are not working in a hermetic room with no relation to the outside – you are one with the overall space and the various dynamics that happen in it."

Effet de serre (Tunis, Tunisia)

The forgotten greenhouse standing in the botanical garden of the Parc du Belvédère in Tunis, Tunisia, was barely on the map when visual artist Farah Khelil "made the mad bet to restore it [back in April 2019] and employ it to create an immersive installation." Claiming that her "gesture was intuitive and experimental, although on a monumental scale,"[143] Khelil started applying for artistic grants with the idea of financing the refurbishment of the whole shattering structure.[144] After two years of work – disrupted by the outbreak of COVID-19 and other toing and froing – the fully refurbished semi-circular metal structure finally welcomed, in the winter of 2021, the artist's artwork entitled *Effet de serre* (meaning *the greenhouse effect*, in French), of which both the polytunnel and the plants it now shelters are intrinsically part of.

As the curator of the installation, Clélia Coussonnet, explains: "*Effet de serre* is a conceptual, committed and critical gesture of renovation of the municipal greenhouse of the city of Tunis in the Parc du Belvédère, which questions the definition of the work of art, the place of the artist and the role of cultural institutions. It shows the emancipation of the artistic gesture from the demands of the market by deviating a grant to aid artistic production towards an action of general interest." A gesture that, unfortunately, as Khelil herself underlines has been hardly understood by the "conservative" cultural and social spheres. Describing the project as "an experimentation within the public space,"

143 Personal conversation, May 2022.
144 In the frame of her project *Effet de serre*, Khelil received the support of AFAC – The Arab Fund for Arts and Culture, Goethe Kultur, 32BIS, CEMAT and CAORC.

Coussonnet sees the greenhouse as an "offering"[145] to the city dwellers as well as a momentum. The hope being that the structure – which will outlive the temporary exhibition – will help revive an area of the park that had fallen into disuse by offering a place where local associations, busy raising environmental awareness at the Parc du Belvédère, could organise workshops and "take the time to inhabit the greenhouse. I'm sure that the Association of Friends of the Belvédère will bring this place to life," says the artist, although she admits *a posteriori* not being fully concerned by the future of the structure. "I never thought of keeping track of my passage. The future of this place will be a marker of the behaviour and mode of existence of its inhabitants, users and owners. I just put it there and that's it. What interests me are the questions that arise from such an experimental project. It's like a research lab. It doesn't give answers but it asks the questions – good or bad, it doesn't matter. It's the issues that come to the surface that I find interesting to observe."

145 For the idea of the 'aesthetic of the gift', see the work of Lewis Hyde, Jacinto Lageira and Marcel Mauss among others.

Growing Resilience

d-o-t-s in conversation with Simon Ronceray[146]

Located in the small French town of Yèvre-la-ville, near Orléans, Les Trois Parcelles is a 60 hectares farm growing and processing a great variety of grains, vegetables and red fruits. It is run by Simon Ronceray together with a collective of nine persons (including Mathilde Oms-Etienney and Valentin Riehm – his future associates – and seven employees). Applying the principles of agroecology, the team employs diversification and land restoration to develop a resilient model capable of positively impacting the farm's social and environmental surroundings. A model in which the judicious use of greenhouses plays a key role.

d-o-t-s What is Les Trois Parcelles?

Simon Ronceray Les Trois Parcelles is a project that I started with my cousin in 2019. At the time I was working in urban agriculture, and he worked in the field of viticulture. We truly wanted to become *paysans*[147] – this job was meaningful to us! We started growing vegetables and cereals on a piece of land that measured 0.8 hectares, and then increased that

146 Conversation originally in French, recorded via WhatsApp on May 24th, 2023.

147 *Paysan, agriculteur*... in French, several words can be used to translate the word farmer. In France the term *paysan* – literally meaning *peasant* – suffered negative connotations, and was often used with disdain, as an insult throughout the 19th and 20th century. (Source: Barral, P., "Note historique sur l'emploi du terme 'paysan'", *Études rurales*, No. 21, (1966), 72-80). Reappropriated by some farmers, the word now carries political meaning: It is generally opposed to the word *agriculteur* and to the capitalist model of a standardised agricultural system that does not take into consideration the specificities of a landscape (know-hows, hydraulic capacities, qualities of the soil, geography, local breeds, endemic plants...) and instead grows the same crop (e.g. maize), or raises the same commercial breed (e.g. Large White pig, Saanen goat) anywhere.

to 4 hectares in 2021. Today Les Trois Parcelles covers a surface of 60 hectares; in January 2022, in fact, we took over the farm of a neighbour who had retired. Since the beginning, the idea was to move from the production of cereals – a common practice in our region – towards the implementation of a diversified agriculture. The challenge with the transition from a monocultural system to an agroecological practice is the reconstitution of the ecosystem. First you need to restore the soil. In our case, the levels of organic matter on our plots were very low, as the soil was destroyed by the former production methods. The other challenge involved is the return of biodiversity, something we accomplished quite quickly thanks to the planting of trees and shrubs with an agroforestry approach and the establishment of plant cover.

d-o-t-s Tell us more about the idea of diversification which is at the heart of your approach.

SR Behind the idea of diversification is the importance of producing enough food to eat all year around. We have what we call a 'greedy' approach in the sense that we want to be able to eat what we produce. This is impossible if we limit ourselves to the production of grains – without processing them into final products such as flour, bread, etc. This is why we started growing several varieties of the same species of vegetables and producing a large variety of red fruits, as well as aromatic herbs. Thanks to this diversity, our clients' dishes are healthy, look pretty and taste nice! Economically speaking, this approach allows us to offer diversified high value veggie boxes with both strawberries, for instance, and vegetables (two types of products that do not compete with one another) and to produce more finished products such as flour and pasta. By doing so, our clients will generally buy both. While this allows us to better amortise billing costs, irrigation costs, delivery costs, etc., it also makes it possible to offer real consistency to people who come to buy from the farm directly. As onsite they can find vegetables, but also meat or eggs, they don't have to drive to many different shops (something common in rural areas) and this limits their carbon footprint.

When harvesting grains, little to no organic matter is extracted from the soil itself. When growing vegetables such as salads, one needs to remove the whole plant from the soil in order to pick it. So in order to renew this lost organic matter, diversity is important. Trees are vital in such a system as they nourish the soil with their leaves as autumn comes. Diversity from an agronomic point of view is therefore very relevant because it assures us good harvests. From an agricultural perspective, diversification is also interesting when it comes to the management of our facilities. With such a system we limit the drop in production in all of our ateliers. The advantage is that when an atelier is not working, we can concentrate on another instead of trying to maintain one at any cost. This is made possible by the fact that we do not use any pesticides on the farm – even those authorised by by the European organic labelling system. As such, we accept the idea of losing some crops as we do not wish to go 'against nature'. We are very focused on weeds – we weed a lot! – but we do not use any substance that we would not put on our plates. Baking soda, white vinegar and black soap are the only products we allow ourselves.

Finally, diversifying is also important in terms of what I call 'food landscape': the idea that the landscape around us should be as beautiful as the ingredients we put on our plates. What I like to give as an example is the milk carton that – with the cute illustration of cows grazing on an hilly landscape – cultivates the idea of happy cows in green pastures. Yet, if the packaging of products found in supermarkets were to illustrate the agricultural reality behind industrially produced milk – that is a closed barn with the cows inside – consumers would be shattered!

d-o-t-s There are several greenhouses installed on the 60 hectares you cultivate. What do you use them for? Are they important for your project's resilience?

SR We have several secondhand polytunnels onsite, as well as a large greenhouse with straight edges and fixed with concrete of 500 square metres. We use it as a nursery for our seedlings. And we just reinstalled three strawberry tunnels. These tunnels enable early ripening of our fruits and vegetables and so the lengthening of the warm season. They allow us to increase the production per square metre – which makes our farm more profitable – and to produce a greater diversity of vegetables in tune with the seasons: the idea being to provide boxes that are varied enough to make people want to be in an AMAP[148]. Our goal is for our customers to continue eating organic vegetables in autumn and winter without having to consume only winter vegetables (beets, carrots, etc.) which, in the long run, can be boring.

d-o-t-s In one of your posts on Instagram, you talk about how greenhouses are important to extend the production period and consequently to "stabilise employment and promote activity in winter to create full-time jobs year-round"[149] and thus revive the villages near the farm. Can you tell us more about this re-peopling mission?

SR From a purely agricultural and business management point of view, overall, seasonal work is very complicated in human terms: people are rarely truly involved. It is also time consuming to train

148 AMAP is the acronym for "Association pour le Maintien d'une Agriculture Paysanne" [Association for the Maintenance of Peasant Agriculture]. Promoting community-supported agriculture, an AMAP is a partnership between a group of people and a farm. Each side is bound by a contract of engagement. The consumers will generally receive a veggie box once a week. In exchange the farmer guaranties ethical ingredients/products – often organic.

149 Instagram post dating from October 28th, 2022. ◊ www.instagram.com/p/CkQ0KPGNRJq/?hl=en (Accessed: May 23rd, 2023).

new people every year. Given the scale of the territory, seasonal workers, generally, do not stay more than 6 months, which means that they are seldom part of the local cultural fabric (musical activities, associations...). Thanks to the greenhouses we extend our diversity of production in winter which means work too. It is therefore possible to fix employment a little better, and thus limit the use of seasonal workers.

d-o-t-s As you mentioned, most of your tunnels are secondhand. The latest was "dismantled and installed onsite in less than a month," as you explain in the Instagram post quoted above. The structure, you reveal, "comes from a French farm that stopped growing seedlings and will from now on stock up in The Netherlands." How do you feel about this globalised production and export of seedlings? Why is it so important for you to grow your own?

SR It is important for us to grow our own plants from scratch because the diversity of varieties we work with is such that only a few or no suppliers can meet our needs. By growing our own seedlings we are also hoping to reduce our charges and our carbon emissions. I would rather buy seeds and compost – which are delivered on pallets – than have a semi-empty truck deliver young plants that take a big amount of space. Growing our own seedlings also supposes that we are free to stop growing young plants any time during the year, instead of relying on a supplier who will require that we subscribe to their services or prepay. By being autonomous, our production of plants is therefore always adapted to our capacity as we go along.

d-o-t-s Recently, we have been reading a lot about so-called 'smart greenhouses'. We are talking here about large heated structures that use LED lights night and day, and employ more and more soilless growing systems. These greenhouses are extensively found in countries such as The Netherlands and some of the arguments in their favour are that they reduce the need for pesticides, and that they can secure our society's food security. What is your position on this?

SR I don't believe at all in the model of these large greenhouses. They convey the idea that with them you can reduce the use of pesticides, but when you look at their energy costs and the plastic they employ, you realise that they are all but virtuous. To me it is like putting a small bandage on a big wound. This system will last as long as there is access to cheap energy. Yet, we know very well that this is already not the case: we saw it with the COVID-19 pandemic and the war in Ukraine. The best way to be resilient is not to depend on this cheap energy-intensive system, but instead, defend a model of society in which the human workforce is valued. I prefer to imagine lots of people working together in small infrastructures, with manure, and chatting over a coffee at lunchtime, sharing experiences and bringing a territory to life!

d-o-t-s In the Loiret area, like in many other regions in Europe and in the world, you have had to deal with record temperatures in recent years. Sometimes, these are also accompanied by very low temperatures in May and June, little to no rain, devastating storms and violent winds which cause a lot of damage to crops and infrastructures (in particular to polytunnels). How does the climate crisis impact your crops, your mental health, as well as your choices and ways of doing things?

SR In the context of Climate Change, tunnels are a godsend, because they provide protection from the cold, hail and strong winds. By acting as a barrier, they limit the process of evaporation of water. Once whitewashed, the greenhouses also make it possible to create a shade net in summer and thus protect our plants from too much sunshine. Our harvests were impacted rather positively last year: the fact that it is very hot allows plants to grow quickly — as long as we have access to water. There are also fewer diseases in organic farming when it is dry and hot than when it is humid, as is generally the case in our region. In itself, we could almost see Climate Change as a positive factor. The main issue for us is the access to water. Water must be managed and conveyed, and this is very demanding physically. Ultimately it weighs on our mental health, especially because we are also profoundly anxious about the changing world, a fear that is not specifically linked to our job, but rather to the fact that we are taking seriously the environmental shock that is coming.

Keep Digging

an essay by Claire Ratinon

My partner has a habit of browsing Facebook Marketplace when he's procrastinating. There are a lot of strange things for sale on the internet. In the autumn of 2020, he found an advert for a full collection of BBC/Time Life *The British Empire* magazines – all 98 issues, from "The Dawn of Empire" through to "King Sugar's Bitter Bequest", being sold by a man clearing out his loft in Pevensey, in the south of England. We picked them up the same day in exchange for a £20 note, and spent that evening flicking through each dusty copy, the ink rubbing off onto our fingertips. In the issue titled, "Presence That Changed The World", I found an illustrated map covered in drawings of plants, animals and four men wearing turbans labelled 'Indians', all linked by orange arrows, set out beneath a sketch of the greenhouses of Kew Gardens. The image of their infamous Palm House sits at the top of the page where the British Isles would have been. The map is titled 'Nature Reshaped' and it depicts how, using a handful of examples, the British Empire rearranged the natural world in hungry pursuit of wealth, land and power. It shows that mongooses were brought from India to the Caribbean, that donkeys were transported from Ireland to South Africa, and that rubber, quinine and oil palm were taken to Kew Gardens to be cultivated, propagated, studied and sent back out to the colonised lands upon which exploitative, extractive, ecosystem-altering economies could be proliferated throughout the world.

Growing up, I wasn't much interested in history and I wasn't much interested in plants. The history I was taught at school was entirely disconnected from who I understood myself to be and the outdoors held no allure to a nerdy child who preferred to spend her days lost in storybooks. I turned away from the notion that any labour that would muddy my hands and knees could be something to aspire to. It may never have been explicitly declared so, but I knew that what was expected of me – as the child of Mauritian immigrants who both moved to England before their twentieth birthdays – was to aspire to work that rose above the lowly and humble act of farming. Our families hoped that we would take the world of opportunity that they had created for us and use it to ascend – socially as well as economically.

I found my way to plants in America where I'd ended up living in an attempt to embrace the status of perpetual foreigner that had haunted me since childhood. I stumbled upon a rooftop farm in New York City and was instantly captivated by this unfathomable place, growing crops in the middle of the city. A remarkable undertaking. After the years I'd spent working in the media, the world of plants – a world I hadn't yet contemplated the existence of – revealed itself to me. Learning the art of growing edible plants was a revelation. I can barely believe I spent so many years ignorant of its alchemy. On a mass of land that was stolen from its indigenous inhabitants and was colonised by the English is where my food growing journey began, and I had to return to England, where I was born so that I could learn and train in the practice that I felt called towards.

Back in London, I took any job I could find that would bring me closer to the natural world and keep my days free of desks and computers. I taught children how to sow seeds in primary schools and community centres, tended rooftop beehives in the centre of the town, and grew salad in implausibly small spaces to feed to the people of Hackney. And while I was growing and studying, I found myself wondering about the forces that shaped the world I had stepped into. Who'd created the curriculum and written the books that I was learning from? Where did the plants that I was growing originate? And how did they find themselves to be on the same patch of earth that I was pushing the tines of a garden fork into?

In organic farming, the answer to almost all of your growing questions is organic matter – compost, well-rotted manure, leaf mould. When your questions about agriculture and horticulture move beyond the practical and meander into the historical, the answer to almost all of your questions is colonialism. When we become curious about the story of the humble potato or the leaves in a quintessentially English cup of tea or dare to wonder how extractive, monocultural systems of agriculture were developed and became so widespread, or consider the possibility that the reason so many people have little or no access to land (and thus no relationship to it) is because a small number of individuals and families hoarded it over centuries, while amassing the power and wealth that land ownership confers – all roads lead our inquiry back to the colonial project.

Colonialism shaped agriculture and horticulture, and colonialism reshaped the natural world. It took plants and animals and humans, and it moved them from place to place, and in doing so, altered (what we still insist on calling) nature irretrievably. Greenhouses – and the botanical gardens that they sat within – played a pivotal part in that. Long before they were re-imagined and re-conceptualised as spaces of leisure, botanical gardens were the colonial tools of European science and imperialist plunder. Plants were torn from the land – stolen, smuggled, shipped – and the ancestral knowledge of the indigenous communities that stewarded the earth in which they grew was appropriated for profit, and the facts of this pillage were erased. Whether they were taken for ornamental horticulture or transported, studied, acclimatised and deployed into the agriculture of the oppression that was practised on plantations around the world, plants were a crucial part of the colonial project. Their forced migrations, re-naming, the erasure of their stories and dismissal of their origins is mirrored in the way in which colonial systems of oppression treated the Black and Brown people who they exploited, and my ancestors were among them.

I am a descendent of slavery and indentureship on the island of Mauritius. Working the land, for me, is not a neutral act. There was no way that I was ever going to devote myself to the work of growing plants without becoming curious about whether the spontaneous compulsion to cultivate the soil and grow plants was fated. Although I put plants into the soil of a land that is, at best, ambivalent about my being here, I happen to believe that I was called to do it. I believe that this practice was meant for me and that the instincts, the inclination, the sense of deep and unbounded connection that I have felt through touching hand to earth, is an ancestral inheritance that reaches past the times when my ancestors were forced to migrate from their homelands, and back to the moments when they were intimately connected to a piece of land that they would have called home.

When I look again at that illustrated map of the world, I imagine the thousands upon thousands of other orange arrows that aren't represented here: the rosy periwinkle whose seeds were taken from the rainforest floor in Madagascar, before being renamed by colonial botanist Carl Linnaeus and whose active compounds are now used to formulate medicines that treat cancer while their flowers bloom in English gardens every spring; the okra seeds defiantly braided into the hair of the West Africans who were forced to cross the Atlantic Ocean in chains; the manioc from Brazil that was brought to the then Isle de France (now Mauritius) by Mahé de La Bourdonnais to keep the enslaved and the oxen from starvation. The many, many living things – the organisms, plant matter, seeds and human beings – that were forcibly moved along these trajectories remain, for the most part, invisible in our agricultural and horticultural institutions. The botanical gardens, the seed catalogues and the garden centres rarely speak of the horrors that their present-day existence is built upon.

I look from the map into the garden behind my house. I look at the hibiscus, cotoneaster and hydrangea whose presence in the gardens of Europe is a manifestation of the colonial project. I look at myself and see that I am a manifestation of the colonial project too. I imagine myself standing on the map next to the greenhouses of Kew Gardens, only 16 miles from where I was born, and see the orange arrows attempting to depict my ancestry flowing back to Mauritius, and then from there to Madagascar, South India, Mozambique, Sri Lanka and beyond. To the many places from which my ancestors likely came.

There is no way that I could do the work of growing plants and choose to ignore the ways in which it intersects with my identity. Despite how the act of working the land carries the trauma and narratives of colonial oppression that persist to this day, it is a radical act of reclaiming a connection to the earth and the natural world, which I insist is my birthright.

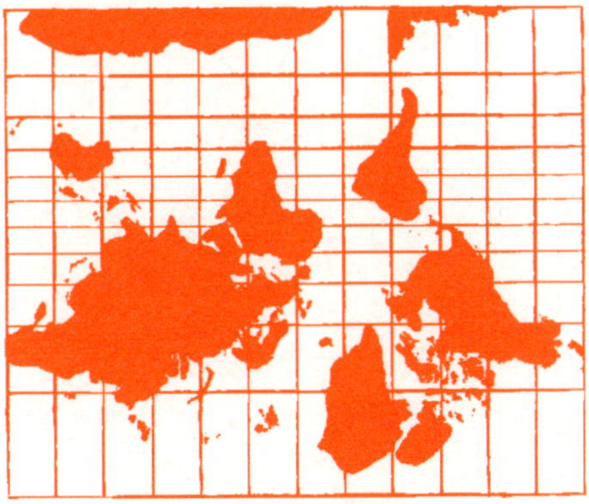

Annex.

A Story from Luxembourg

Before becoming this book, *Greenhouse Stories* was an ephemeral event that, between 2021 and 2022, took place inside a semi-abandoned horticultural complex in Soleuvre, Luxembourg. In collaboration with creatives and associations from different backgrounds, the greenhouses that populated the site were transformed into an ever-changing and unconventional cultural space. The following pages retrace this experimental curatorial project and recall the various actors who took part in it.

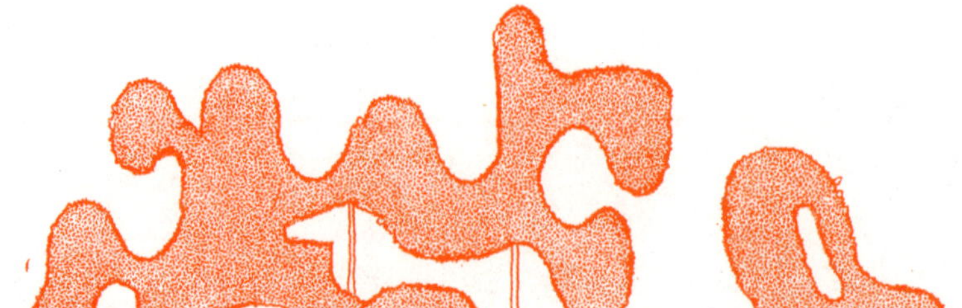

An Exhibition-laboratory to Cultivate New Ideas

words by d-o-t-s

In the summer of 2020, Italian curator Anna Loporcaro invited us to develop a project for *loop — down the hills, across the land*, an artistic programme that she was conceiving for the municipality of Sanem (Luxembourg) as part of *Esch 2022 — European Capital of Culture*. The concept behind *loop* was that of a walking itinerary through various areas of the town along which a series of art and design installations, as well as temporary events, would engage the audience under the overall motto 'Remixing Culture'. While the core programme took place from June 22nd to July 21st 2022, all the invited participants were given nearly two years to develop their concepts and root them as much as possible in the existing context.

During our first site visit, in September 2020, we were shown various potential locations for our intervention and, among them, was an horticultural complex located in the quiet residential area of Soleuvre. [imgs. 1,2] Almost entirely covered by spontaneous vegetation, the ensemble featured several glasshouses and two polytunnels. Overall, the buildings were in good shape, although full of objects and waste that the last owners had left behind. [imgs. 3 – 5] Once the headquarters of a flourishing horticultural business, we learnt, the site had just been purchased by the Sanem municipality after 10 years of abandonment with the long term plan of tearing it down and make space for a series of housing units. The place — with its story and contradictions — seduced us.

From a curatorial point of view, it offered us, in fact, the platform to test working methodologies that we had been eager to explore for a while. On a theoretical level, could the greenhouses reveal dynamics worth expressing in an exhibition? On a practical level, intervening in a non-institutional site presented opportunities and challenges — in terms of content production and public engagement — that we were not familiar with and that we were keen to put to the test. The fact that the horticultural complex was at risk of being dismantled added an extra layer of stimulation to the whole: could we think of a project capable of showing to the decision-makers of the city that more creative and open futures for the greenhouses of Soleuvre were imaginable and achievable?

We thus embarked on a creative journey to rethink what the site could become and which dynamics it could trigger and support. The founding intention was that of transforming the greenhouses into an ephemeral cultural space, a permeable and hybrid laboratory dedicated to the cultivation of new ideas and spontaneous encounters through exhibitions, workshops, performances and conferences. The major challenge would be to turn the purely functional glass architecture — a 'machine' built to grow plants — into a welcoming and engaging environment — a cosy space, attractive enough for passersby to stop and frequent. We also thought it would be important for our intervention to be able to tell the site's story, respecting the building and highlighting its peculiar features. With their translucent structures — semi-open to the outside — the glasshouses naturally encouraged us to reason in terms of transparency (in the sense of *honesty*), inclusion and mediation. We welcomed that 'suggestion' and developed our project around a series of guiding principles.

What mattered the most to us was to materialise a certain approach to exhibition-making, one entailing a militant take on pressing environmental and social issues, the conscious and senseful use of materials for the construction of the scenography, and the engagement of non art/design-savvy audiences. The discussed topics should be approached from a glocal[150] perspective and we should

150 For a definition, see: Blatter, J., 'glocalization', in *Encyclopedia Britannica online*, February 22nd, 2022. ◊ www.britannica.com/topic/glocalization (Accessed 30 January 2023).

find ways of creating connections between international examples and the Luxembourgish context. The exhibition should constitute the occasion for us to empower young creatives whose work we appreciated and found thought-provoking. The accompanying cultural programme should generate conversations and bottom-up proposals with the involvement of communities from different horizons and ages. And, of course, the project's ultimate goal should be that of freeing the greenhouses from their fate (i.e. being demolished); in that sense, the whole intervention should find ways of nourishing a sentiment of affection for the site, inviting the local population to take an active role in its reactivation and preservation.

We had roughly 20 months to put the entire project together and, to achieve what we had in mind, a variety of people needed to be involved from the beginning, and on a continuous and long-term basis: the selected artists and designers – so that we could conceive together pertinent and contextualised projects; the inhabitants – so that they could have enough time to apprehend the space and its potential; the local associations and schools – so that we could integrate them in the cultural programme in meaningful ways; and the various teams of the municipality – so that they could accompany us all along, taking care of key safety and restorative measures. Multi-layered and plural, the concept that originated from our reflections tried to make sense of the numerous self-imposed conditions as well as existing infrastructural limitations, and revolved around three main areas of intervention: the greenhouses as a curatorial subject; the greenhouses as an exhibition space; the greenhouses as a community activator.

The greenhouses as a curatorial subject

We decided that greenhouses – not the ones hosting us, but greenhouses in general – would be the subject of the exhibition mainly for two reasons. On the one hand, we found it important that this new project constitute a continuation of the critical discourse we had proposed with our previous endeavour, the touring show and publication *Plant Fever*, which looks at design from the perspective of plants, considering them as more than passive beings (or materials) that we can take for granted. We wanted this new project to become a second chapter of our investigations into human-plant relationships. On the other hand, presenting an exhibition *about greenhouses, inside greenhouses* would allow us to observe empirically some of the dynamics we aimed to address in the exhibition and the accompanying publication (i.e. the book you are holding in your hands).

We thus approached the research, building upon the knowledge and the other-than-human perspective that we had acquired when developing *Plant Fever*, and kick-started our endeavour looking at a series of references that we had collected then and that we believed could help us set the tone for the narratives we now wished to assemble. This also helped us define the typology of works we should look for and present in the show.

Among the others, we found Monica Gagliano's words on greenhouses particularly powerful and stimulating. In her book *Thus Spoke the Plant*, Gagliano defines them as symbols "of colonialist approaches of subjugation and oppression," and as perpetrators of "the objectification of plants as pure commodities within a capitalist model of production and consumption."[151] The 19th-century gardening manual *Every Lady's Guide To Her Own Greenhouse, Hothouse, and Conservatory*, written in 1851 by an anonymous British 'Lady' – in which the author presents greenhouses as safe spaces for women where "there is nobody to question [their] judgement, nor condemn [their] acts" – was also key in helping us establish a radical posture on the topic.

What interested us, in fact, was the possibility of developing an exhibition capable of revealing some of the controversies that greenhouses embed and represent, going beyond their celebration as technical prowesses and

151 Gagliano, M., *Thus Spoke the Plant* (Berkeley, California: North Atlantic Books, 2018), 92.

exceptional architectural feats – aspects that have already been widely explored in the botanical and design realms. This made all the more sense, we believed, when considering greenhouses from multispecies and post-colonial perspectives, but also as tools potentially contributing to the ongoing climate crisis and Western society's loss of connection with the soil.[152]

Keeping that in mind, our early investigations led us to the identification of four main topics that, because of their contemporaneity and their capacity to spark meaningful debates, could form the core of the exhibition: the paradoxes of the cut flower industry – with a focus on the production of roses in Kenyan polytunnels; the intensive cultivation of fruits and vegetables – with a focus on the eco-social landscape of the Mar de plástico, in Spain; greenhouses as spaces for the emancipation of women – looking at past and present examples of female growers empowered by the act of gardening; greenhouses as tools for the colonial appropriation of flora – with a focus on the plant-box known as the Wardian case. Beside their relevance on an international scale, these four subjects gave us the opportunity to create strong connections with the Luxembourgish context. In some cases because of historical similarities, and in others because of the possibility of using them to engage the local population through participatory processes.*

The greenhouses as an exhibition space

Following ten years of abandonment, some of the greenhouses of the horticultural complex in Soleuvre were not in an optimal state and presented several safety issues. Not all of them were therefore apt to receive an audience, and the municipality granted us access only

152 On the idea of "loss of connection with the soil", see the notion of *hors-sol* (literally *off the ground*), brought forward by contemporary French thinkers such as the late Bruno Latour, Malcom Ferdinand and Baptiste Morizot.

* For more information about the addressed topics and the featured projects, see the dedicated sheets at p. 195-211.

to two of them (plus a small garden). [imgs. 6 – 8] While at first we saw these space limitations as a handicap for the project, they quickly became the occasion for us to reflect more deeply on our responsibilities as cultural agents and which of the unwanted consequences of an ephemeral intervention like this could be avoided. Very often, in fact, the production of temporary design exhibitions entails the creation of waste – either because of the lack of time to carefully plan material cycles, or because of solutions (e.g. special supports and displays) that are not conceived to be disassembled or reused elsewhere or elsewhen. In our case, the 20 months we had to prepare the project afforded us enough time to think and do things differently. To try to palliate to the footprint of the exhibition, we thus decided to fully embrace the non-institutional character of the greenhouses, using them as a material library and a laboratory. While the municipality of Sanem was responsible for reconditioning the buildings – repairing the numerous leaks, securing the glass ceilings, and installing essential services such as composting toilets and the access to water – we invited the French duo Radeau Studio (Elodie Chabert, Zélie Canouet) to conceive the show's scenography.

Because of the aforementioned space limitations, we imagined the exhibition as a series of consecutive thematic installations, each lasting one week and dealing with one of the four selected topics. Featuring exhibits as diverse as perfumes, large-format photos, films, archive materials, textiles and fragile objects, the installations should also serve as the starting points for dedicated conferences and hands-on activities. The request to Radeau Studio was therefore to develop the scenography as a modular kit capable of answering specific technical necessities, performing multiple functions and providing an ever-changing perception of the same space. [imgs. 9 – 12] In addition to be easily mountable and dismountable by two people, the elements produced by Chabert and Canouet were also to be thoughtful in terms of materials employed – both at the moment of sourcing and at the end of their life.

Embracing these constraints, the duo managed to develop a simple, flexible and dynamic display system made of attentively repurposed 'ingredients' found in the greenhouses[153] and collected from other locations and partners.[154] Beside fulfilling their tasks, the furnishings and the scenographic devices developed by Radeau Studio acted as physical repositories of some of the greenhouses' technical features, and highlighted the multiple creative possibilities of elements normally considered as waste and leftovers. [imgs. 13 – 17] During the exhibition period, the resourcefulness manifested by the scenography became itself a conversation starter, stimulating meaningful discussions with specialists (designers, architects, circular economy specialists, curators...) and the general public about the goings-on behind the production of an exhibition and the ways in which we can operate otherwise, making such events more resource-conscious.

The greenhouses as a community activator

Parallel to the technical aspects linked to the refurbishment of the glass-houses and the production of the scenography, the challenges of converting the complex into a durable cultural hub involved also its re-appreciation within the urban and social fabric. After ten years of neglect, passersby were in fact either accustomed to perceiving it as a 'dead' site or were unaware of its existence at all. How to ensure that people would now *see* the greenhouses and consider them as an open space that they could freely attend and whose transformation they could be part of? Bringing people onboard – efficiently conveying the message that the horticultural complex belonged to the community, and was accessible to everyone – was probably the most difficult part of our undertaking. The greenhouses needed to be put 'back on the map', and enough attention and curiosity had to be generated so that the neighbours and the wider public would

153 Glass frames, metal tubes, plastic and metal hooks, horticultural nets...
154 Among the others: European linen textile samples from CELC's storage (Paris, France); leftover plywood from an art installation of designer Olivier Vadrot (Beaune, France); carpet from the Réserve des Arts' storage (Marseille, France).

step inside them. This, we believed, should be done humbly and cautiously. In this sense, we asked French graphic design studio Structure Bâtons (Lucile Bataille, Sébastien Biniek) to care for the visual identity of the space with subtle yet inviting interventions. [imgs. 18–21] Our intention, in fact, was not to produce a big one-off spectacle that would storm the location and quickly fade away, but rather create a project that, through small-scale impulses — a sort of acupuncture process, really — could establish a meaningful and long-term relationship between the community and the site.

Reactivating the greenhouses via a rich and inclusive cultural programme, we thought, was the best way to achieve this. Partnering up with local associations, schools, neighbours, and international artists, we put together an agenda of events as diverse as hands-on creative workshops, food design experiences, conferences and debates, music and dance performances, gardening and foraging classes, exploratory walks... On the one hand, such disparate activities were meant to captivate audiences of various backgrounds — children and adults, professionals and amateurs, classes and families — adopting *learning by doing* and embodied forms of knowledge transfer, and calling for their active contribution. On the other hand, the diversity of these events enabled us to test the flexibility of the space, providing the community and the decision-makers of the city with 'suggestions' regarding the multiple uses that such a non-institutional and non-standard site could be employed for culturally-wise — a fertile environment open to everyone's imagination. [imgs. 22–27]

The technical rehabilitation of the horticultural complex in Soleuvre was made possible largely thanks to the engagement of C.I.G.L. Suessem, a non-profit organisation that works with unemployed people, helping them reintegrate into social life. In the spring of 2021, their teams cleared up all the waste present onsite — which, in total, amounted to eight construction dumpsters — and put back in function the two large polytunnels and the multiple cultivation beds. Since then, the organisation has been using the site to cultivate organic fruits and vegetables — strawberries, tomatoes, courgettes, green beans, fennel, potatoes, aubergines, salads... — that are then distributed free to the local schools, retirement homes and associations. The work of C.I.G.L. Suessem was directly and indirectly beneficial to our project, and we established fruitful collaborations that involved our combined skills of agricultural professionals and cultural actors.

As previously stated, saving the greenhouses from being demolished was the primary objective of our whole intervention and, in that sense, creating a movement of people that would come forth and fight for the survival of the greenhouses was essential. The various events were therefore a recurrent occasion for us to meet personally with the local inhabitants, share our intentions with them and collect their inputs. Being physically present onsite during the entirety of the project was key and, between the autumn of 2021 and the summer of 2022, we spent a total of 78 days living and working inside the greenhouses. Among others, two moments were particularly relevant and powerful in terms of exchange with the public: the launch of the project and its finissage.

In October 2021 we officially started our physical intervention in the greenhouses through a two-week residency during which we organised an 'open-house weekend' with guided tours of the site and workshops for families. This constituted the first time in 10 years that people were allowed to enter the complex again. During the two days, curious neighbours came to rediscover it and shared with us anecdotes and rumours about its previous existence (i.e. the time when the glasshouses were a family-run flower business). The stories they told us about – which spoke of an era of tireless activity, and a place run with passion – and the tone they employed – a mix of melancholy and regret – nourished our narrative and somehow confirmed the responsibility we had in bringing the greenhouses back to life. Nine months later, at the end of July 2022, we organised the finissage of the exhibition in the form of a 'giveaway'. [img. 28] Over two days, we opened the greenhouses one last time and everything – from the furnishings and the scenography elements built by Radeau Studio to the numerous pots and other horticultural tools and materials we had found in the complex, as well as the plants that we had sowed and cared for – was distributed free to the visitors. It was a festive moment attended by many of the people – families, artists, associations... – who had contributed to the project or who had simply taken part in the events we had organised.

The finissage also marked the symbolic transfer of the enterprise to the local community: After almost two years since the beginning of our project, it was now time for the neighbours to take things forward.

***

The greenhouse learnings

The reactivation of the horticultural site in Soleuvre is, for a number of reasons, one of the densest and most meaningful curatorial endeavours we have carried out so far. Curating 'from the inside' – living and working with/in the greenhouses – we were able to observe first-hand some of the issues we were tackling in our theoretical investigations, such as the fast-paced production of vegetables, the fact that these structures are often deadly traps for insects and birds, and the light pollution they generate. [img. 29] At the same time, as a hybrid and permeable space, the site opened up possibilities of audience engagement that would not have been possible in a traditional cultural venue: from the experimental format of many installations and events, to the participation of people who are generally less accustomed to frequenting artistic places. Moreover, what the greenhouses potently reminded us is that curation can be understood and practised as a powerful act of care and activism. The kind and variety of questions and comments that the project produced reaffirmed, in fact, the potential role of exhibitions – if we care to build them in that sense – as living platforms through which we can shape radical worldviews, raise critical questions and mediate social, political and environmental issues. A strong *sense of purpose* is what we will keep forever with us from this project.

p.s. To our great surprise and satisfaction, in November 2022, the municipality organised a 1-day workshop led by the Luxembourgish cultural project manager Séverine Zimmer (the coordinator of the loop — down the hills, across the land *artistic programme) during which local inhabitants, decision-makers, gardeners and architects gathered to analyse what we had done during our intervention and what could be done in the future to secure the durability of the greenhouses. A charity shop, a collective drying room for flowers, a plant nursery, a repair café, an experimental eco-habitat, and using the buildings' roofs to collect rainwater were among the scenarios discussed for the potential repurposing of the whole complex or parts of it. While the feasibility and success of these plans will depend largely on the political agenda of the next city council — and it is still definitely not sure that the outcome will be positive — we are happy to see that the seeds that we planted in 2021 grew into something worth fighting for. Especially in a context that, by definition of its own inhabitants, is generally not so receptive to grassroots projects.*

1

2

3

4

5

6

7

8

9

10

11

12

13

14

15

16

17

18

19

20

21

22

23

24

25

26

27

28

29

Four Art Installations to Look Critically at Greenhouses

words by d-o-t-s

Conceived as an ever-changing exhibition, *Greenhouse Stories* (June 22nd – July 21st, 2022) proposed looking at greenhouses as controversial [agri]cultural production tools. Four temporary art installations analysed as many topics – the rose industry; the production of fruits and vegetables; the emancipation of women; the colonial appropriation of flora – trying to create bridges between international case studies and the Luxembourgish context. Featuring the work of young professionals from various creative backgrounds, the installations invited children and adults to discover and question the identity and history of greenhouses. While some of the projects and materials exhibited already existed prior to the show, some others were specifically commissioned from selected designers and were realised partly through collaborative processes.

22.06 – 26.06.2022

The Fragility of the Rose

From Luxembourg's Broken Dreams to Kenya's Collapse: When the Rose Industry Trembles

Between the end of the 19th century and the middle of the 20th century, the Luxembourgish rose industry thrived. Mainly established in the Limpertsberg district (Luxembourg City), a series of family-run commercial nurseries developed varieties of blossoms that were exported all over the continent to enrich the gardens of the European bourgeoisie and nobility. A testament to the importance of the rose economy for the self-proclaimed 'Country of Roses' was the 1925 International Exhibition of Paris in which Luxembourg participated with a pavilion in the shape of a rose garden.

The predominantly French consumer base, however, rendered the country's flower economy poorly armed against political changes. When World War I erupted and France stopped buying products from states of the Deutsche Zollverein – to which Luxembourg belonged – the country's rose production almost came to a halt. The spread of the *phylloxera* – an invasive pest attacking wines that affected all plant exports through Europe – did not help the Luxembourgish rose-related economy, which eventually stopped completely with the outbreak of World War II.[155]

Almost a century later, in the spring of 2020, it was the turn of Kenya – one of the early 21st century's top global rose producers – to witness the fragility of the cut flower industry. With the explosion of the COVID-19 pandemic, the African country faced a sudden and significant reduction of flower purchases from Europe, its main market.

Before the health crisis, rose production provided work to over 100,000 people (many of them women), and an average of 30 flights left Nairobi, the country's capital, each day to deliver the flowers to European customers. By mid 2020, those numbers had drastically dropped: Kenya's exports declined by 85%, many farmworkers lost their jobs, and tonnes of unsold roses were left rotting.[156]

155 For more information regarding the production of roses in Luxembourg, ◊ patrimoine-roses.lu/.

156 Sources: Fredenburgh, J., "The 4,000 mile flower delivery", *BBC online*, 2019. ◊ www.bbc.com/future/bespoke/made-on-earth/the-new-roots-of-the-flower-trade/ (Accessed: September 4th, 2021); Faux, Z., Herbling, D., Munsterman, R., "The Crash of the $8.5 Billion Global Flower Trade", *Bloomberg online*, April 16th, 2020. ◊ www.bloomberg.com/features/2020-flower-industry-crash/ (Accessed: September 4th, 2021).

FEATURED PROJECTS

The Scent of Economic Loss

by Coltrane McDowell

Coltrane McDowell was in Kenya when the pandemic broke out. While witnessing the collapse of the country's rose industry, the Canadian designer also saw an opportunity: to turn the otherwise wasted scented blossoms produced by a local rose farm of the Mount Kenya region — where McDowell grew up as a child — into a precious and lasting product that would provide growers with an alternative income. The result was a perfume entitled *The Scent of Economic Loss*, which crystallised an unprecedented historical moment and highlighted the fragility of the globalised flower economy.

DATE	MATERIALS
2020	Perfume, perfume diffuser, video (10:25)

Roses of Luxembourg: An Archive

with Patrimoine roses pour le Luxembourg

Long forgotten, the history of the Luxembourgish roses has been dug out by Patrimoine roses pour le Luxembourg, an association of rose collectors and amateurs active in the country. Their research has highlighted the historical importance of this industry both locally and internationally — unveiling for instance the complex networks of rose growers, as well as the infrastructures (e.g. glasshouses) it required.

LENDERS

— Nicole Trossen-Gilson (Patrimoine roses pour le Luxembourg)

— CNA Centre National de l'Audiovisuel Luxemburg

ARCHIVE MATERIAL

Catalogues, stamps, postcards, posters, excerpt from the movie *De Lampertsbierg* (directed by Joy Hoffmann and Misch Bervard, produced by CNA Centre National de l'Audiovisuel, Luxemburg, 2021)

29.06 – 03.07.2022

Europe's Vegetable Garden

Mar de Plástico: Behind the Scenes of Spain's Controversial Agricultural Business

Located in the Spanish province of Almeria, the Mar de plástico (*sea of plastic*, in Spanish) is the largest greenhouse-covered area in Europe. Enveloping a surface equal to approximately 50,000 football fields, the region – which is described as one of the most recognisable things from space – owes its name to the endless landscape of white polytunnels that local farmers use to grow food year-round. The white tarps are employed to reflect sunlight and protect the crops from the summer heat and strong winds.

Accounting for 40% of Spain's total agricultural exports, the Mar de plástico produces each year a dazzling 3.5 million tonnes of vegetables and fruits – from peppers and tomatoes to cucumbers and melons. More than 60% of these products (some of which are labelled as 'organic') end up on the shelves of European supermarkets such as Tesco, Asda, Carrefour, Lidl and Aldi. Praised by the Spanish government and the major players of the European agri-food sector as an "economic miracle,"[157] the Mar de plástico's feat has been taken as an example by other states – like California – that are looking for cost-effective cultivation systems in water-scarce environments.

However, the local production is far from guiltless. Stories of human right violations and pollution are documented regularly. Harvesting the area's fruits and vegetables are, for instance, many illegally-employed migrant workers from Senegal, Morocco or Ukraine. Paid as low as 35 euros/day, these workers are frequently exposed to pesticides and high temperatures and live in precarious settlements, often with no running water and electricity. It is also their appalling working and living conditions that enable European consumers to buy and eat cheap products.[158]

157 See: Christ, M. K., *This Garden of the Sun: A Report on Almería's Miracle Economy* (2013). ◊ www.scapegoatjournal.org/docs/05/SG_Excess_364-371_P_CateChrist.pdf (Accessed: September 9th, 2021); De Pablo, O., Zurita, J., Kelly, A., Carlile, C., "'We pick your food': migrant workers speak out from Spain's 'Plastic Sea'", *The Guardian*, September 20th, 2020. ◊ www.theguardian.com/global-development/2020/sep/20/we-pick-your-food-migrant-workers-speak-out-from-spains-plastic-sea (Accessed: September 10th, 2021).

158 Rippingale, J., "Consumers are not aware we are slaves inside the greenhouses", *Aljazeera online*, October 16th, 2019. ◊ www.aljazeera.com/features/2019/10/16/consumers-are-not-aware-we-are-slaves-inside-the-greenhouses (Accessed: January 15th, 2021).

FEATURED PROJECTS

Mar de Plástico
by Simon Lenskens

Back in 2015, Belgian photographer Simon Lenskens went to Almeria to record the reality hidden behind Spain's massive agricultural business. Documenting the harsh everyday life of migrant workers and portraying landscapes dominated by infinite plastic tunnels, the series of photographs that Lenskens brought back with him tell the story of a system based on human exploitation, overproduction, waste and pollution.

DATE	MATERIALS
2015	Print on cotton textile

Transvegetal intuitions
by Iñaki Cancillo Mora

Mixing archive footage and quotes from contemporary philosophers, the video essay by Spanish architect Iñaki Cancillo Mora is an invitation to question the way we humans have domesticated Nature and have put the vegetal realm under our control in large greenhouses and other monocultural systems.

DATE	MATERIALS
2021	Video (3:35)

Un-wrapped Dinner
by Giulia Soldati & Téa Laurent

Devised as a performative dinner, the project by culinary designers Giulia Soldati and Téa Laurent reflects on the role of food as a medium to convey stories otherwise difficult to hear and swallow. Drawing from anecdotes and facts, Soldati and Laurent have devised a menu that brings the guests on a sensorial journey unveiling what happens underneath the white polytunnels of the Mar de plástico.

DATE	MATERIALS
2022	Textile, ceramic, food, sound

Initiated and commissioned by d-o-t-s for *Greenhouse Stories* in 2021, *Un-wrapped Dinner* is a temporary event that took place on July 3rd 2022.

06.07 – 10.07.2022

Ladies Do What Ladies Want

Women & Greenhouses: Cultivating Empowerment

Back in the 18th and 19th centuries in Europe, outdoor gardening was considered a man's discipline. However, botany and domestic gardening figured on the list of accomplishments that (wealthy) girls were encouraged to master.[159] Confined to their homes, many young women felt empowered by the relative freedom that this knowledge and practice offered them.[160]

Evidence is the many manuals written by female gardeners published during the period. Among them was *Every Lady's Guide To Her Own Greenhouse, Hothouse, and Conservatory*, a short gardening essay written in 1851 by an anonymous English 'Lady'. In it, the author recounts her joy of tending to indoor plants, and gives practical information on how to build a greenhouse and which specimens to grow in such an environment.

Describing the greenhouse as an antidote to monotony and boredom, the 'Lady' highlights the empowering feeling of "being mistress of [her] own greenhouse," as one can "do as [she] pleases" and "there is nobody to question [her] judgement, nor condemn [her] acts."[161]

***

Nowadays, women around the world are still empowered by the simple act of gardening. Be they professional growers, groups of activists collectively managing a piece of land or ordinary women harvesting homegrown vegetables, they share a similar quest for autonomy and freedom.

159 Rousseau, J-J., "Lettres élémentaires sur la botanique", in *Collection complète des œuvres*, Vol. 7 No.4, (Genève: Du Peyrou et Moultou, 1780-1789) ◊ www.rousseauonline.ch/pdf/rousseauonline-0048.pdf last edited on October 7th, 2012 (Accessed: April 6th, 2021).

160 Sparke, P., *Nature Inside: Plants and Flowers in the Modern Interior* (New Haven: Yale University Press, 2020).

161 *Every Lady's Guide To Her Own Greenhouse, Hothouse, and Conservatory,* by a Lady, (London: W. S. Orr & Co Paternoser Row, 1851). ◊ books.google.fr/books?id=VE8DAAAAQAAJ&pg=PA1&source=gbs_toc_r&cad=4#v=onepage&q&f=false (Accessed: November 16th, 2020).

FEATURED PROJECTS

Des mots sur des serres

by Structure Bâtons

The result of a series of letter exchanges with female gardeners from all over the world, the project by graphic design studio Structure Bâtons consists of a collection of embroidered textile banners. Evoking the protest panels used by women's rights activists in the 19th century, the textiles act as visual repositories of memories, impressions and sketches dealing with freedom, resilience, transmission but also love and death.

DATE
2022

MATERIALS
Textile, digital embroidery, postcards

Des mots sur des serres is a project initiated and commissioned by d-o-t-s to Structure Bâtons in 2021 for *Greenhouse Stories*

Send us
news of your
garden!

I feel the trust
when growing
plants and flowers
an art of caring
and building

13.07 – 17.07.2022

Decolonising Ward's Case

From Appropriation to Appreciation: Rethinking the Colonial Plant-box

Before the advent of steam engines, being able to efficiently and securely trans-port live flora over distances was a big challenge and, over the centuries, human communities (e.g. the Lapita people, in Oceania, around 1000 BCE)[162] created various ingenious tools and techniques to succeed in their endeavours.

Among the devices developed over time, plant-boxes were the most employed by European colonial empires in the 18th and 19th centuries. Also known as 'miniature greenhouses', these small structures – essentially wooden cases sealed with glass panels – allowed Europeans to appropriate exotic plants, medicinal herbs and economic crops (e.g. bananas, indigo and cotton) and move them from one continent to the other. The sealed environment of the boxes permitted, in fact, the carrying of the specimens on boat trips that could last several months protecting them from adverse conditions (e.g. saltwater and low temperatures), but also insects, rats and cats.

In the 19th century, British doctor and plant enthusiast Nathaniel Bagshaw Ward managed to popularise his own version of the plant-box which would then be referred to as the 'Wardian case'. Cost-effective and easy to produce, his device was quickly adopted by some European nations who used it extensively to impose unbalanced power relations on other peoples and ecosystems. The case was also instrumental in enabling colonial powers to establish questionable behaviours with the vegetal realm such as plant hunting, plant looting (biopiracy) and more generally the reduction of plants to mere commodities.[163]

162 For more information about the Lapita people's inventions to transport plants on long trips, see "Telling Stories with Plant Cases", the essay written by Adriana Craciun at p. 65 in this book.

163 Sources: Keogh, L., *The Wardian Case: How a Simple Box Moved Plants and Changed the World* (Chicago: University of Chicago Press/Kew Publishing, 2020); Teltscher, K., *Palace of Palms: Tropical Dreams and the Making of Kew* (London: Picador, 2020); Bagshaw Ward, N., *On the Growth of Plants in Closely Glazed Cases* (London: John Van Voorst, 1842).

FEATURED PROJECTS

Souvenirs of Plants
by dach&zephir

Once a symbol of colonial power, in the hands of French designers Florian Dach and Dimitri Zephir, the Wardian case becomes a hybrid device that favours the observation and poetic "capture of plant memories." By subverting the cultural and technical codes embedded in the original object, the duo propose a more respectful exploration of the plant realm: one based on curiosity, creativity and respect.

The installation was complemented by artefacts and films created by the participants of a week-long workshop led by dach&zephir in Soleuvre, Luxembourg, in May 2022.

DATE
2022

MATERIALS
Aluminium, stainless steel, rolpin plywood, sycamore maple, caning, rattan, pla, polycarbonate

Souvenirs of Plants is a project initiated and commissioned by d-o-t-s to dach&zephir in 2021 for *Greenhouse Stories.*

Natalya Ayers is a floral artist, florist and grower. Formerly based in Scotland – where she co-founded the botanical studio PYRUS – she recently relocated to Liguria, Northern Italy, to establish a new botanical studio and regenerative growing project. Together with special creative projects and events, she will welcome people to learn and create in the olive terraces and pastures of the beautiful, but latterly underpopulated, mountain villages of Imperia.

Luis Berríos-Negrón is a Puerto Rican environmental artist and experimental architect working with the forms and forces of global warming. He is Associate Professor and Research Fellow at Umeå University, Sweden. *Of Tree Nurseries, and other Possible Forms of Phenomenotechnical Geoengineering* is the working title of his current research, which stems from an investigation into the national post-hurricane reforestation project of Puerto Rico.

Adriana Craciun is the Emma MacLachlan Metcalf Chair of Humanities at Boston University. Her most recent books are *Writing Arctic Disaster: Authorship and Exploration* (Cambridge University Press, 2016), and with Mary Terrall, *Curious Encounters: Voyaging, Collecting, and Making Knowledge in the Long Eighteenth Century* (University of Toronto Press, 2019). She is completing a book on plant longevity and botanical collecting, *Arctic Enlightenments: Deep Time Floras and the Svalbard Global Seed Vault.*

d-o-t-s is a nomadic curatorial practice founded by Laura Drouet and Olivier Lacrouts. The duo's investigations focus on the diverse and questionable relationships that human communities establish with other animals, plants, and landscapes. Defined by the participatory and interdisciplinary approach, d-o-t-s' work spans writing, exhibition-making, hands-on workshops and design commissions.

Charlène Flores is a photographer whose work shows the environmental issues plaguing her native region, Brittany (France). Among others, her reportages have documented the proliferation of toxic green algae on the Breton coast and the negative effects on living beings of light pollution provoked by commercial greenhouses. Formerly based in Hong Kong, she has recently moved back to Brittany to be a political advisor to local policymakers.

Monica Gagliano is a Research Associate Professor of Evolutionary Ecology at Southern Cross University (Lismore, Australia) and Director of the Biological Intelligence Lab funded by the Templeton World Charity Foundation, where she studies intelligence in non-neural organisms and specifically decision-making, learning and memory in plants. She is the author of *Thus Spoke the Plant* (North Atlantic Books, 2018).

Prudence Gibson's research is informed by theoretical concepts of plant studies, eco-feminism, sustainable art & design and post-human theory. Her work extends to scripting and producing video art, narrative projects and curatorial approaches to plants. She is the author of *The Plant Contract* (Brill, 2018) and *Janet Laurence: The Pharmacy of Plants* (NewSouth Books, 2015). Her new book is *The Plant Thieves: Secrets of the Herbarium* (NewSouth Books, 2023).

Fiona inglis is the co-founder of PYRUS, a botanical design studio established in 2011 in East Lothian, near Edinburgh (Scotland). Inspired by the landscape, seasonal rhythms, scent and poetry PYRUS produce botanical designs and installations for brands, events and creative producers championing local and seasonal materials, mostly grown in the studio's Victorian walled cutting garden.

Téa Laurent is a designer interested in the notion of commensality and the power of food to generate encounters between different ethnic groups. Focusing on the *gens du voyage* – the Travellers community to which she belongs – her projects span mobile kitchens, installations and performances in the public space, and aim at giving voice to people who are generally hidden in our standardised cities.

Simon Lenskens is a Belgian photographer. In 2017 he completed a Master's degree in Visual Arts Photography at the Royal Academy of Fine Arts in Ghent, Belgium. The topics that particularly fascinate him are mostly of a social or political nature. Through his photographs he investigates some interesting statements made by the media and whether they can be regarded as true or not. Within this research, Lenskens attempts to tell a new story about his own experiences with the people he photographs.

Michael Marder is IKERBASQUE Research Professor in the Department of Philosophy at the University of the Basque Country, Vitoria-Gasteiz (Spain). His writings span the fields of ecological theory, phenomenology, and political thought. He is the author of scientific articles and monographs, including *Plant-Thinking* (Columbia University Press, 2013); *The Philosopher's Plant* (Columbia University Press, 2014); *Hegel's Energy* (Northwestern University Press, 2021); *Green Mass* (Stanford University Press, 2021) and *Philosophy for Passengers* (The MIT Press, 2022).

Coltrane McDowell is a designer, artist, and writer whose work is preoccupied with context and how the designer's point-of-view can be deconstructed. His projects often take the form of poetic visual stories and are the results of sensitive community engagement. In 2020, McDowell graduated cum laude from the Social Design master course at the Design Academy Eindhoven (The Netherlands) and is currently based in Basel (Switzerland).

Joanna Moreno Michels is a French independent journalist based in Almeria (Spain). Her work focuses on the condition of migrant workers in Andalusia, with particular attention to issues linked to migration, modern slavery, and the inconsistencies and damages of the local agro-industry. She is also a contributor to the bulletin of the international organisation, European Coordination Via Campesina ('The collective voice of peasant farmers in Europe').

Claire Ratinon is an organic food grower and writer based in Britain. She has grown edible plants for restaurants, schools and community spaces in London, and delivered talks for organisations including the Royal Botanical Garden, Edinburgh. She is the co-author of *Horticultural Appropriation* (Rough Trade Books, 2021), and the author of *How To Grow Your Dinner Without Leaving The House* (Lawrence King Publishing, 2020). Her second book is *Unearthed* (Chatto & Windus, 2022).

Simon Ronceray is the co-founder of Les Trois Parcelles, a 60 hectares farm located in Yèvre-la-Ville (France), the village where he grew up as a child. The son and grandson of farmers, he holds a degree in agricultural engineering. Before starting Les Trois Parcelles in 2019, he worked for three years in the field of urban agriculture, collaborating with the Parisian association Veni Verdi.

Penny Sparke is a Professor of Design History and the Director of the Modern Interiors Research Centre at Kingston University London (UK). She conducts research around modern design and the modern interior with a special interest in the role of gender. Her latest book is *Nature Inside: Plants and Flowers in the Modern Interior* (Yale University Press, 2021).

Structure Bâtons was co-founded in 2014 by Lucile Bataille and Sébastien Biniek. The projects developed by the duo span graphic design, curation, workshops, educational tools, type design, and publications. Focusing on different peoples, their folklore, and their visual constructions, the research by Structure Bâtons is nourished by teaching activities, collaborations, and residencies.

Kate Teltscher is a cultural historian and writer. Her most recent book is the acclaimed *Palace of Palms: Tropical Dreams and the Making of Kew* (Pan McMillan, 2021). She is the author of *India Inscribed* (Oxford University Press, 1997) and *The High Road to China* (Bloomsbury Publishing, 2007, shortlisted for the James Tait Black Memorial Prize for Biography). She is an Emeritus Fellow at the University of Roehampton, Honorary Research Associate of the Royal Botanic Gardens, Kew, and Fellow of the Royal Historical Society.

Ken Walczak is a researcher, educator, designer and artist. He studied film and photography and owned 801 Design – a furniture and lighting design company. Since 2008 he has focused on engineering, science and student outreach at the Adler Planetarium in Chicago, designing innovative instrumentation for research. Recent projects include underwater meteor retrieval, an orbital satellite, stratospheric exploration and ground-based light pollution observations.

Colophon

d-o-t-s wish to thank:
all the contributing authors, Francesca Anfossi, Natalya Ayers, Stéphanie Bertel, C.I.G.L. Suessem, Iñaki Cancillo Mora, CELC (Odile Idkowiak, Laur Thouverez), Clélia Coussonnet, dach&zephir (Florian Dach, Dimitri Zephir), Charlie Drouet, Eis Epicerie, Lucile Farin, Marie Fischer, Charlène Flores, Quentin Hiernaux, Fiona Inglis, Sabrina Kamili, Farah Khelil, Sophie Krier, Elisa Laird, Téa Laurent, Pascal Lazarus, Simon Lenskens, Anna Loporcaro, Laura Maggi, Coltrane McDowell, Joanna Moreno Michels, Municipality of Sanem (and in particular Cliff Schmit and Steve Ginepri), Giulia Quattrini, Radeau Studio (Zélie Canouet, Élodie Chabert), Onomatopee (Cecilia Casabona, Jesse Muller, Natasha Rijkhoff), Laurence Rodriguez (Cirad), Simon Ronceray, Services for Creatives (Séverine Zimmer, Valentina Arnò, Anna Becker), Giulia Soldati, Structure Bâtons (Lucile Bataille, Sébastien Biniek), Tox the Fox, Nicole Trossen-Gilson, Deborah Tyler, Olivier Vadrot, Ken Walczak, Harry Watkins, and everyone who contributed [knowingly & unknowingly] to the research and production of this project...

Concept & editing	d-o-t-s (Laura Drouet, Olivier Lacrouts)
Contributing authors	Luis Berríos-Negrón, Adriana Craciun, Monica Gagliano, Prudence Gibson, Téa Laurent, Michael Marder, Claire Ratinon, Penny Sparke, Kate Teltscher
Design & illustrations	Structure Bâtons
Translations	d-o-t-s
Proofreading	Deborah Tyler
Photography	Coltrane McDowell [pp. 85–101], Simon Lenskens [pp. 103–117], Charlène Flores [pp. 119–139], loop // Olly Cruise, Steve Ginepri, Services for Creatives, Mike Zenari [pp. 177–211]

Onomatopee 245
Greenhouse Stories: A Critical Re-examination of Transparent Microcosms
by d-o-t-s (Laura Drouet, Olivier Lacrouts)
—
ISBN: 978-90-833621-0-6
Onomatopee Projects, Eindhoven NL
Jesse Muller and Natasha Rijkhoff
www.onomatopee.net
—
1st edition, 2023, 1250 copies
Printing: As Printon, Tallin
Paper: Inside — Munken Print White 90g; Cover — Munken Lynx 300g
Fonts: Media 77 (Optimo), Doodah (Structure Bâtons)
—
No AI was used at any moment for the writing of this book